DEVELOPMENT CENTRE

POLICY REFORM, ECONOMIC GROWTH AND CHINA'S AGRICULTURE

by
Christopher Findlay, Will Martin
and
Andrew Watson

DEVELOPMENT CENTRE
OF THE ORGANISATION FOR ECONOMIC CO-OPERATION AND DEVELOPMENT

ORGANISATION FOR ECONOMIC CO-OPERATION AND DEVELOPMENT

Pursuant to Article 1 of the Convention signed in Paris on 14th December 1960, and which came into force on 30th September 1961, the Organisation for Economic Co-operation and Development (OECD) shall promote policies designed:

— to achieve the highest sustainable economic growth and employment and a rising standard of living in Member countries, while maintaining financial stability, and thus to contribute to the development of the world economy;
— to contribute to sound economic expansion in Member as well as non-member countries in the process of economic development; and
— to contribute to the expansion of world trade on a multilateral, non-discriminatory basis in accordance with international obligations.

The original Member countries of the OECD are Austria, Belgium, Canada, Denmark, France, Germany, Greece, Iceland, Ireland, Italy, Luxembourg, the Netherlands, Norway, Portugal, Spain, Sweden, Switzerland, Turkey, the United Kingdom and the United States. The following countries became Members subsequently through accession at the dates indicated hereafter: Japan (28th April 1964), Finland (28th January 1969), Australia (7th June 1971) and New Zealand (29th May 1973). The Commission of the European Communities takes part in the work of the OECD (Article 13 of the OECD Convention).

The Development Centre of the Organisation for Economic Co-operation and Development was established by decision of the OECD Council on 23rd October 1962.

The purpose of the Centre is to bring together the knowledge and experience available in Member countries of both economic development and the formulation and execution of general economic policies; to adapt such knowledge and experience to the actual needs of countries or regions in the process of development and to put the results at the disposal of the countries by appropriate means.

The Centre has a special and autonomous position within the OECD which enables it to enjoy scientific independence in the execution of its task. Nevertheless, the Centre can draw upon the experience and knowledge available in the OECD in the development field.

Publié en français sous le titre :

RÉFORME POLITIQUE, CROISSANCE ÉCONOMIQUE
ET AGRICULTURE EN CHINE

*
* *

Foreword

This study is one in a series of case studies commissioned in the context of the 1990-92 work programme of the OECD Development Centre on "Developing Country Agriculture and International Economic Trends" under the direction of Ian Goldin.

ALSO AVAILABLE

Agricultural Trade Liberalization. Implications for Developing Countries *edited by Ian Goldin, Odin Knudsen.* Series Development Centre Seminars (1990)
(41 90 04 1) ISBN 92-64-13366-6 FF180 £18.00 US$32.95 DM60

Biotechnology and Developing Country Agriculture: The Case of Maize *by Carliene Brenner.* Series Development Centre Studies (1991)
(41 91 14 1) ISBN 92-64-13595-2 FF100 £13.00 US$24.00 DM39

The Future of Agriculture: Developing Country Implications *by Martin Brown, Ian Goldin.* Series Development Centre Studies (1992)
(41 92 02 1) ISBN 92-64-13628-2 FF160 £20.00 US$38.00 DM62

Investing in Food *by Ruth Rama.* Series Development Centre Studies (1992)
(41 92 08 1) ISBN 92-64-13747-5 FF220 £32.00 US$55.00 DM90

Prices charged at the OECD Bookshop.

THE OECD CATALOGUE OF PUBLICATIONS and supplements will be sent free of charge on request addressed either to OECD Publications Service, or to the OECD Distributor in your country.

Table of Contents

List of Tables, Figures and Boxes

Acknowledgements

The authors gratefully acknowledge the financial support of the Finnish and Swiss governments for the Development Centre's country studies, the assistance of the Rockefeller Foundation in facilitating the Bellagio meeting in which the project's findings were reviewed, and the comments of Ian Goldin on successive drafts. The opinions expressed in this study are the sole responsibility of the authors and do not necessarily reflect those of the OECD, or any other institution or government.

Some of the research by Findlay and Watson reviewed in this paper was originally supported by a grant from the Australian Research Council.

Preface

Structural adjustment and trade liberalisation are matters of immediate and deep concern for all those interested in economic development. Research carried out within the OECD Development Centre's programme on Developing Country Agriculture and International Economic Trends aims to provide fresh perspectives which may facilitate the reform process.

The Centre's research on agriculture incorporates several components: a conceptual component to provide analytical guidance for the broader issues; a global general equilibrium model to analyse the overall trends and policy consequences; a component to analyse the links between economic reform and technological change in agriculture; and a series of country case studies, of which this is one, to look at the reform options and their implications for individual representative countries. This study provides analytical insights into the interactions between macro-economic and trade policies and agricultural development in China.

China is a giant, and in coming years is expected to become an even more significant force in shaping the course of global economic and human development. The reform of the Chinese economy has attracted special interest for two major reasons: first, because of the implications of the transformation of economic relations for domestic production, income and food security; and second, because of the implications of these developments on the rest of the world.

This study reviews the progress of the reforms already undertaken, drawing lessons for the future. In emphasising the interactions between trade, macro-economic, agricultural and other sectoral reforms, the study draws on a general equilibrium model of China developed by one of the authors. The study concludes that further reform of agricultural product pricing and the international trade system in the short term would raise China's agricultural self-sufficiency. However, in the longer term, reform and the associated rapid economic growth and structural change will have the effect of reducing self-sufficiency. The process of transformation will be facilitated by a sequencing of the reform process which places greater emphasis on the liberalisation of external trade and the exchange rate regime. The findings thus provide an empirical and model-based complement to the 1990 Development Centre Study by Kym Anderson, which shows that long-term comparative advantage in China is moving away from agriculture into manufacturing sectors.

In the depth and breadth of its analysis, its sensitivity to detail and its novel methodological approaches, the study will recommend itself to Chinese policy makers. The economy-wide approach to Chinese agricultural development, together with the consideration of the implications for the overall development of China and its external impact, make it of interest to a wider audience.

Jean Bonvin
OECD Development Centre
January 1993

Executive Summary

The Spread of Reform

The major elements of the post-1978 rural reforms were the reintroduction of household farming and free markets in the Chinese countryside, and the implications of these changes for rural investment and non-agricultural enterprises. Our analysis of the evolution of household farming and the free retail and wholesale markets demonstrates how each phase of economic development after the original changes of 1978 created strong pressures for further reform. What started out as a reform of the system of labour management and of agricultural prices led to the collapse of collective farming as managerial decisions were decentralized to the household. This, in turn, stimulated the growth of free markets which challenged both the state price structure and state controls over the distribution of agricultural products. The influence of the free markets fed back into production by encouraging specialization, and forward into distribution by generating wholesale trade. This also began to affect urban-rural exchange. The economic forces generated in this way then proceeded to change the structure of rural investment and led to a new phase of rural economic growth based on the development of rural enterprises. The process of agricultural reform thus developed according to its own economic logic and could not be kept within discrete areas.

Reform Cycles: the Market vs. Administrative Control

Such changes heralded a change in China's rural development strategy away from the former preoccupation with pure agriculture and local self-sufficiency towards a diversification of production based on regional comparative advantage and an integrated approach, involving all sectors and relying on the market as a resource allocation mechanism. Needless to say, this has entailed major political and institutional adjustments. The subordination of economic activity to governmental administration has begun to give way to a pattern where economic linkages no longer coincide with the pattern of administrative control. The bureaucratic system is thereby losing its ability to play a direct role in controlling economic flows. Inevitably, this is a political issue. While administrative obstacles to economic movement across boundaries remain, and while local officials remain unwilling to relinquish all of their economic powers (or retain those powers disguised as new forms of ownership, licensing and taxation), the free market system is not yet fully free to follow its own logic of development. In effect, both the party and government hierarchies have to change their structures and adjust to using indirect methods of influencing market systems without preventing the markets from performing the functions now required of them. Where the markets began both to challenge the economic and political authority of the party, the authorities have felt compelled to reassert greater administrative controls. This led to cycles in the process of reform over the decade.

Reform is Incomplete

Common aspects of the process of reform were cycles of deregulation and the reinstatement of controls, and the 'balkanisation' of many agricultural markets. This problem of barriers to inter-regional trade tends to exaggerate the instability in urban markets, reinforcing the cycles of reform and re-regulation. The origins of the barriers to inter-regional trade lie in the partial nature of the reforms. One example is the different rates of deregulation in various markets which leads to a continued bias against raw materials production compared to processing, and the incentives this creates for local governments to intervene in order to protect local interests. Another example is the devolution of power in an international trade system which retains the administrative mechanism of quantity targets.

The reform process is far from complete. Further reforms include:

- the removal of internal barriers to trade, associated with various commodity wars, which will promote the pursuit of regional comparative advantage;
- the development of marketing institutions which will also promote the development of national markets for agricultural products;
- access to new varieties of grains and other technical inputs which will raise yields;
- more secure land tenure and land transfer arrangements which will facilitate the structural adjustments in agriculture following the rural industrial boom.

There is scope for substantial increases in productivity associated with further agricultural reforms in China. Agricultural product prices were low (in the second half of the 1980s) compared to world prices. Price reforms would therefore have also added to growth in agricultural output. Reforms up to the mid 1980s had certainly generated an impressive growth in agricultural output. Those growth rates slumped in subsequent years, recovering again in the late 1980s and early 1990s. The recovery this time was due to a combination of policy changes (higher prices) and good luck (the weather and its effect on yields). The contribution of price changes to output growth is not surprising, given the extent of the taxes on agricultural producers that applied in 1986. The benefits of the first round of reforms had continued to be taxed heavily through highly distorted prices. It took price changes in the late 1980s to kick along agricultural output again. But further institutional reforms are also possible.

Impacts on Agricultural Self Sufficiency

Economy-wide policies also have important implications for agriculture. The reforms to the international trading system have prompted the rapid increase in the international orientation of the Chinese economy, and even though substantial trade barriers remain, there is now a closer matching of China's comparative advantage and trade patterns. The expectation in a relatively resource-poor economy such as China is that in the long run the share of agricultural products in exports will fall and that agricultural self-sufficiency will also fall. These longer-run forces can be illustrated by the effects of a rural industrial boom, or a change in factor endowments or growth in incomes. The former pair of changes are shown to have relatively large impacts on the degree of agricultural self-sufficiency compared to the impacts of income growth on demand (via different income elasticities).

The short-run impacts of further reform could, however, be different. The combination of policies specific to particular commodities, and the effects of the exchange rate system, have taxed both exporting and import-competing parts of the agricultural sector. The dynamic effects of growth are likely to lead to further price reforms (and removal of sector-specific price distortions) as the balance of forces in the political economy of policy-setting changes.

Agriculture and Macroeconomic Management

Agriculture is also affected by the macroeconomic management of the Chinese economy. In general over the 1980s, the macroeconomic performance of China was impressive. However the process of decentralisation that was an integral part of the reforms led to some problems of macroeconomic imbalances. The institutions for macroeconomic control are still under development in China. The instruments that are used (credit controls, price controls) can have direct impacts on the rural sector and on agriculture. In addition, the distortions associated with these sorts of intervention and with the exchange rate system also mean that macroeconomic changes can have effects on the pattern of rural production which reduce welfare and growth. These occur not only because of the differential income elasticities of demand, but also because of an important nominal rigidity in the Chinese economy, that is, the exchange rate. Small changes in macroeconomic variables can have substantial impacts on trade patterns in particular.

Summary

In summary, China began the rural reforms with what in hindsight were the easier things to change, for example, the degree of household responsibility. Output growth boomed as the rural economy 'caught up' to its production possibilities. Once those productivity gains were exhausted, however, there were highlighted another set of reform issues, especially land tenure and price distortions. Furthermore, the end of the first stages of reform coincided with an increasing difficulty of controlling the Chinese macroeconomy. The greater swings in macroeconomic performance had substantial impacts on the mix of agricultural output. These problems highlight another reform agenda about money and foreign exchange markets. The agricultural sector (and China's agricultural trade partners) have just as much interest in these issues now as in price distortions and other aspects of land management. The original reforms generated a dynamic force of their own, which despite the presence of the reform cycles, prompted the trend towards the increasing reliance on markets as resource allocation devices. The same sorts of forces are likely to generate pressure for reforms to deal with the outstanding issues.

Chapter 1

Rural Reform and the Impact of the Market on Chinese Agriculture

1.1 Introduction

This chapter provides an overview of the process of rural reform in China and examines the way in which the evolution of market relationships affected Chinese agriculture. It demonstrates how the introduction of household farming and limited free markets had a profound impact on the structure of the rural economy and set in train a series of economic and institutional changes which led inexorably towards greater reliance on market interaction as the basis for production and distribution. Such changes also had significant social and political consequences. The analysis therefore includes discussion of the political economy of the reforms and of the way it shaped the process taking place. They also reflected a fundamental shift in China's rural development strategy.

In the following sections, we shall first briefly review the introduction and nature of household farming which forms the basis for all other aspects of the reform process. We shall then examine the evolution of market and price reform, which in turn will lead to discussion of the consequent impact on rural investment and non-agricultural activities. This chapter thus provides the foundation for our subsequent analysis of the relationship between growth and structural change, of changes in the production and marketing of particular commodities, and of the general equilibrium model of Chinese agriculture.

1.2 The Introduction of Household Farming

The introduction of a system of production contracting in China's rural communes after 1978 was originally intended as a managerial reform which would increase incentives to peasant farmers and reduce the costs and complexities of collective management (Griffin, 1984; Guo Shutian, 1990a; Watson, 1984 and 1985). Combined with increases in plan prices for agricultural products and limited free markets for the sale of household surpluses, the impact on peasant producers was profound. Responding to the price incentives and marginal freedoms they had gained, peasants experimented with increasing levels of managerial decentralization. Within three years, the contracting system was transformed from one based on collective accounting and collective income distribution, with bonuses for groups of peasants who exceeded their contract targets, to one based on a complete transfer of management of land and labour to individual households. The households paid the collective a tax and a levy in return for the right to farm their contracted land as they liked. In effect, the leaders of collectives no longer played any direct role in the management of agricultural production, and, apart from the land, ownership of all other means of production passed to the peasants. The *raison d'être* of the communes had disappeared, and in 1983 they were disbanded. After more than twenty years in which collective farming and state controls had dominated Chinese agriculture, peasant households once again became the basic unit of agricultural production, organizing their production in response to a combination of demands from the government and signals from the market.

By the mid-1980s, therefore, the key characteristics of the new system of management of production in Chinese agriculture were in place. Land is owned by the villages and contracted to peasant households for farming. The peasants may not sell the land but have the right to sub-contract it to others or to hire labour to farm it, if they do not wish to farm themselves. In return for the land, the peasants agree to pay a tax to the government, to produce an agreed amount of particular crops (essentially grains, cotton and oil crops) to sell to the state system at plan prices, and to hand over a levy (the amount of which varies in different localities) to the village to maintain collective services (the level of which also varies). Apart from land, all other means of production can be owned and managed by the household. Households are free to plan their production as they like and to dispose of their labour and products as they want to, once they have fulfilled their contract. They may accumulate capital and invest it as they choose. They may also withdraw their labour entirely from agriculture and take up other activitities.

Such a fundamental transformation of agricultural production does not, however, mean that the role of the collective and the state has disappeared. The village still owns the land, provides some services and inputs to its members, and, as discussed below, plays a major role in the development of non-agricultural enterprises. The state still manages some of the markets in key commodities through a system of planned purchases at state prices and sales to consumers at subsidized prices. Central and local governments and village leaders thus continue to intervene in household production, using a combination of administrative decisions, management of some markets, and price controls. This combination of household independence, government intervention and free markets, however, has resulted in a complex set of economic relationships. Although active intervention by government is limited to some markets, even that intervention has effects across the whole economy. The large fluctuations in agricultural production during the second half of the 1980s have been one of the consequences. The reform process is thus still evolving, and the general trend is towards increasing the role of the market as the allocation mechanism for capital, labour and products.

The impact of these changes on agricultural production and efficiency after 1978 was striking. The growth rate of agricultural output value increased from 2.9 per cent in the period 1952-78 to 7.4 per cent in the period 1978-84 (Lin, 1989, p. 2). Over the years 1979-89 the average rate was 5.9 per cent (SSB, 1990, p. 51). Growth rates for the production of most agricultural commodities accelerated, with the fastest gains made in the first half of the 1980s. At the same time, the pattern of land use changed, with a diversification of production, a decline in the sown acreage of grain and an increase in the acreage of economic crops. Surplus labour precipitated out of agriculture, and there was a shift of resources to non-agricultural activities.

According to Justin Lin (1989) much of the explanation for these developments can be seen as one-off gains from the institutional reforms. The reintroduction of household farming removed the management costs and administrative inefficiencies associated with the collectives. Households also became sharply aware of their opportunity costs and were free to respond to marginal incentives. Increases in prices and changes in price relativities were thus able to influence peasant behaviour. Existing potential from the investments in land, irrigation and other inputs made under the commune system could be realized, and the incentives to make full use of new inputs of such things as plastics, chemical fertilisers and improved seeds were strong. The combination of institutional changes and of price incentives thus worked to raise the productivity of the factors of production.

Nevertheless, the reforms to date still leave many issues unresolved. A fundamental one centres on the relationship between the plan and the market in the circulation of agricultural products and in the determination of prices for inputs and outputs. The current situation involves both state agencies and free markets, and a combination of planned, negotiated, and free market prices, with some commodities subject to all three. Producers are thus faced with different marketing channels for the same products and a complex set of price relativities. Household farming has, however, given them greater freedom to respond to the signals received, with the result that the output of different agricultural commodities has fluctuated widely and investment of labour and capital has tended to move towards activities generating the largest returns. In this situation, the government has intervened when production of commodities essential for urban consumption and processing has declined or when price rises have provoked reactions from urban consumers. It has tried to enforce production contracts and to influence market flows. It has also used subsidies to producers to encourage production and subsidies to consumers to protect them from price increases. The result has been a cycle of change in which periods of increasing market liberalization have been interspaced with periods of reassertion of administrative controls. While the overall trend has been towards an ever greater role for the market, continued administrative intervention in respect of sensitive key commodities continues to have a major impact on the way marketing and pricing operate.

A second set of unresolved issues involves the nature of property rights and their implications for investment. These are particularly important in respect of land and of non-agricultural enterprises. Land is collectively owned but managed by individual families. The initial contract period of three years inevitably meant that farmers were unwilling to invest in the land and operated with a short time horizon. The contracts were soon lengthened to fifteen years or longer, and most villages now act as if they will remain stable in the long term. Nevertheless, demographic change means that continual small adjustments are made, and land has to be transferred between families. As a result, there are uncertainties in land management which affect household investment decisions and land use. In addition, continuing peasant concerns over the stability of current policies and the absence of a well-established land-renting system tend to obstruct land transfers and land consolidation.

Many non-agricultural enterprises, especially the larger ones, are owned by villages. This means that they remain part of an economic system based upon collective ownership by all the peasants living within a defined area. Since that ownership cannot be realised through a market, as might the case for share-holding for example, the enterprises remain subject to administrative intervention from village leaders, providing them with a source of revenue and enabling them to intervene in economic decisions (Watson, 1992). The result is the development of local economic systems which respond to market signals from the outside but are structured like miniature planned economies internally. While they have developed rapidly and increased local employment and value-added, they also form part of a local network of patronage and protection which can easily hinder the development of integrated national markets and affect the way investment decisions are taken.

Finally, a third set of unresolved issues relates to the system of rural administration. The independence of the household is established but the role of the village in relation to the household is still evolving (Watson, 1992). Discussion within China expresses the issue in terms of 'dual-level management'. It is argued that individual households are too small and fragmented to accumulate and invest in agricultural development and that they require many pre- and post-harvest services. Nevertheless, there is much debate over whether the village collective is the appropriate mechanism to perform these functions. Some observers see this as an attempt to rebuild the communes, with the associated dangers of managerial inefficiencies and costs which provoked the reforms in the first place. Others argue that integrated management functions might be provided through the development of co-operatives or other voluntary organizations among farmers based on economic needs and free from administrative intervention. Such co-operatives might develop horizontal or vertical linkages according to need and would be free to operate across administrative boundaries. Inevitably, this debate has implications for the ideological principles espoused during the collective period. Fluctuations in official policy towards the issue thus reflect the political aims of the party and government. In the post-June 1989 period, much official rhetoric was directed towards reasserting the role of collective village management, and this remains an important emphasis in government policies (CCP Central Committee, 1991). Nevertheless, the underlying tension between household independence and village-level intervention has not changed, and since official policy also criticises the idea that the original form of collective might be restored, the uncertainties remain.

Given the significance these unresolved reform issues, it is not surprising that the system of household farming remains in a transitional stage, requiring, in the words of the party, 'stabilizing and perfecting'. Furthermore, resolution of the above problems raises a number of political issues related to the economic power of party and government organizations, the relationship between local and central governments, and the social position and role of individual entrepreneurs. The way the reforms evolve in these areas will thus have a major impact on the behaviour of peasant households, on the social and economic power of different social groups, and, thereby, on agricultural production as a whole. In the following sections therefore we shall review the process of and prospects for reform in respect of marketing, pricing, investment and non-agricultural rural enterprises.

1.3 Marketing Reform

Marketing reform became one of the major targets of agricultural policy in China with the proclamation of Document 1 in 1983 (the following discussion draws on Watson, 1988). The call by the Central Committee's Document 1, 1983 (Zhongguo Nongye Nianjian Bianji Weiyuanhui, 1983, pp. 1-5) to liberalize the marketing system was, however, little more than acceptance of a process which was already taking place. The introduction of household farming after 1979 and the decline of commune management meant that most peasants were already taking advantage of their freedom to trade their surplus production on local free markets. Households had begun to plan at least part of their production for sale on the market, and a process of specialization and commercialization was under way. This process fed backwards into production by encouraging further specialization and diversification, and forwards into marketing by stimulating the emergence of long-distance trade and specialized markets and merchants. In effect, the market had already began to act as an engine of economic change and growth.

These developments presented a direct challenge to the planned system of agricultural distribution. During 1979-82, party policy had tried to restrict the role of the free markets, keeping them for purely local exchange. By 1983, however, their dynamic growth and the rapid increase in agricultural output which had accompanied this had forced a change. Thereafter, the acceptance of a major role for market relationships in agricultural development became a central feature of agricultural policy. By late 1991, therefore, the party proclaimed that 'except for a small number of major agricultural goods whose procurement and trading are centralized by the state according to regulations, the trading of all other agricultural goods should be decontrolled and regulated by the market' (CCP Central Committee, 1991, p. C1/4). While the free market thus remained controlled in respect of a small number of basic commodities, the rest of agricultural production had been progressively thrown open to market regulation. Furthermore, the party also called for gradual steps 'to reduce the variety and quantity of goods subject to centralized control and to expand the scope of market regulation' *(ibid.)*.

One of the signs of the intensification of China's free market system during the 1980s was the emergence of a national network of free wholesale markets. These not only affected the production and distribution of agricultural commodities, but also had a direct impact on many other economic activities, such as transport, storage, market service industries, communications systems, and commercial banking and financial services. In all these areas, free wholesale markets began to operate outside the planned system and in competition with it. In addition, such markets had important social and political effects. They led to the resurgence of cultural and social ties based on market contacts, and to the development of private merchants who made a living out of the ownership and sale of market commodities. Previously such people had been classed as capitalist speculators and suppressed. Now they were seen as providing an essential service and as playing a positive role in promoting economic efficiency.

The development of free markets in China has thus had major and widespread ramifications, both economically and politically. Two aspects, however, are relevant here. First, their evolution illustrates the inter-related nature of reforms in the agricultural sector. The interaction of household farming, price changes and free market growth meant that the process of rural reform developed an economic momentum of its own. Second, the divergence between economic linkages as expressed through the market and administrative and planning linkages as expressed through the hierarchy of party and government territorial organization, introduced an institutional tension which also demanded continued reform and adaptation. In what follows, we illustrate these two major themes by looking at how the reform of agricultural marketing took place. We begin by briefly reviewing the major features of marketing through the state planned system.

1.3.1 Agricultural Marketing through the State System

Agricultural marketing before 1978 was characterized by a complex set of interlocking institutions and by the existence of distinct channels for the marketing of different categories of products (Donnithorne, 1967, pp. 273-307 and Ma Hong, 1982, pp. 286-300). Furthermore, it is important to bear in mind that the reforms have not totally replaced these institutions, and that they continue to play a role in agricultural marketing. They include the Ministry of Commerce which once controlled all urban commerce, the supply and marketing co-operatives which controlled rural commerce, and the grain departments which were in charge of the purchase and distribution of grains and edible oils. In addition, various specialized import and export corporations handled products required for export or export processing.

Until the reforms began, these four systems formed the major networks for trade in agricultural commodities. Agricultural products not consumed directly in the countryside passed through them, and they formed the main channels of exchange between town and country. As far as possible the distribution of products through these systems was organized according to plan quotas. Small-scale and local products not easily handled in a planned way were managed through a network of trade warehouses run by the supply and marketing co-operatives. These warehouses bought from the peasants and, at regular intervals, held provincial or national conferences to sell their stocks of goods. Supplies and prices were negotiated depending on seasonal production and the nature of demand. In effect, this system provided a slightly more flexible marketing network which compensated for some of the rigidities in the plan network.

The only other feature of the agricultural marketing system over the period 1958-78 was the intermittent operation of a limited number of periodic local free markets, or rural fairs. Until the reforms began, these acted as a medium of exchange between peasant households within a locality. Their chief function was to enable peasants to balance household surpluses and deficits. They played no role in urban-rural exchange, commerce outside their immediate area, or in wholesale marketing. Furthermore, for much of the period after 1958, they were suppressed and their trade was strictly limited. They did not operate in cities and their numbers declined, reaching a low point of around 20 000 in 1976 (State Industrial and Commercial Administration Bureau, 1984).

Within this marketing system, each type of product was handled through a particular network and was subject to a fixed structure of base and surplus prices, according to a regulated system of three product categories (Ma Hong, 1982, pp. 293-96, and Zhongguo Nongye Nianjian Bianji Weiyuanhui, 1983, p. 411). The first category included grains, edible oils, cotton and other commodities deemed to be of key economic or strategic importance. These were subject to unified purchase and sales *(tonggou tongxiao)* and were the most strictly controlled. The second category included such things as pig products, tobacco, medicinal herbs, hemp, silk, tea, wool, fruits, raw lacquer and other products needed for urban consumption and processing. These were subject to a system of assigned purchase *(paigou)* which was meant to be slightly less strictly planned than the first category but in practice were managed in much the same way. Although these two were different in the way quotas were allocated, in the state agencies responsible for administering them and in the way prices were fixed, they were both rigid in operation and consisted of allocated production and sales quotas subject to fixed prices (see section 1.4). From the producers' point of view, they were much the same thing. Finally the third category consisted of local products, less important for urban-rural exchange, which were planned and managed by government agencies at the local level.

Overall, the operation of this agricultural marketing system had four main weaknesses. First, it lacked flexibility. Planned quotas and prices limited local initiative and could not be adjusted rapidly to take account of seasonal variations in conditions. In particular, the efforts made to restrict regional, seasonal and quality price differentials discouraged the development of regional comparative advantage and gave no incentive for investment in improved varieties and handling or in better-quality higher-cost products. Second, the existence of separate hierarchies for different categories of goods, with many intermediate layers in their aggregation and disaggregation, entailed slowness of operation and problems in the handling of perishable and small-volume products. Third, the operation of the system entailed high bureaucratic costs. Finally, and most significantly, the whole structure of marketing was defined by the territorial hierarchy of governmental administration. Marketing networks operated through vertical lines of administration based on political boundaries. These boundaries were not aligned with natural production and transport networks, and the development of economic links across administrative borders was effectively blocked. This lack of freedom for regions to specialize in production and to develop flexible economic interaction was a significant factor in restricting levels of income in rural areas (Lardy, 1983, pp. 175-89).

1.3.2 The Expansion of the Free Market System

The limited liberalization of the free markets introduced in 1979 gradually undermined the foundations of this state marketing system. Households initially gained the right to trade small amounts of sideline production on the local free markets. This right was then extended to include surplus output of all categories of goods once contractual obligations to the state were fulfilled. Alongside these changes, the reforms of agricultural prices discussed below transformed the profitability of different products, depending on the amount sold and the prices applying in the channel through which they were sold. For example, the free market price index expressed in terms of the base state prices for the years 1980-84 shows that average market prices were consistently over 40 per cent higher. For some goods such as grains and edible oils, prices were between 90 and 100 per cent higher (SSB, 1986, p. 147). This ratio remained much the same in 1991 (Guo Shutian, 1991). There were thus powerful economic incentives for peasants to maximize the quantity sold at the highest prices and to produce those products with the highest relative profitability.

Between 1978 and 1985, therefore, the state marketing system experienced a number of radical changes. The state monopoly gave way to a much looser structure whereby the peasants were required to sell a proportion of their output to the state agencies as stipulated in their contracts and were free to trade any surplus output as they wished. The proportion of goods controlled by the state declined and the proportion handled through the market increased. At the same time as these changes were occurring, there was also both a tremendous growth in agricultural output and a strong increase in urban demand for agricultural products. This demand was intensifying as a result of income growth and increasing consumption of better-quality foods. The increase in both output and demand could not be handled efficiently through the sluggish state system, and the rapid growth of the free market network was inevitable. Market centres were hastily established in villages and urban streets, and both individual peasants and collective units began to trade on them. Eventually, as noted above, Document 1, 1983 formally liberalized the marketing network, and in February 1983 the State Council approved new regulations for the management of free markets which loosened controls and sanctioned the types of trading which had emerged (State Council, 1983). The markets were now defined as a 'component part of the unified socialist market'. State units, collectives and individuals were free to trade openly on them, and peasants could become traders and engage in long-distance commerce.

The next phase of major reform came in 1985. Encouraged by the growth of the rural economy, and particularly by the huge grain harvest of 1984, the Chinese government decided to abolish the system of unified purchase and sales for key commodities and to replace it by a contract system. At the same time it was decided to decontrol the market in most other commodities, including meat, fruit and vegetables (CCP Central Committee, 1985). The way these reforms were implemented, however, sent a series of negative signals to the now independent household producers, especially in respect of grain production (Guo Shutian, 1990b, pp. 15-16). The government no longer agreed to buy all grain offered for sale; the proportion of state purchases at higher prices was reduced; state subsidies to rural grain-deficit areas were reduced; the grain tax was converted into a cash tax; and, meanwhile, the prices for production inputs were raised substantially. The net effect was a drop in the returns on contract crops, a marked shift to more profitable agricultural products and a substantial decline in grain output. This was also associated with a subsequent fall in meat production and in the output of other products dependent on grain.

After 1985, therefore, agricultural production and marketing entered a new phase of marked fluctuations. The optimism of 1984 was replaced by a worry that agricultural output and supplies would not meet consumer and industrial needs. During 1986-87, the administration of the contract system for the key commodities of grain, edible oils and cotton was strengthened so that it more or less reverted to a mandatory plan system (Guo Shutian, 1990b, pp. 17-18), though still leaving a secondary market for surplus grain outside the contract. In addition, incentives in terms of the supply of cheaper inputs were provided to encourage farmers to produce more grain, and in subsequent years, state prices were increased to improve profitability. At the same time, the management of other commodities passed to local governments, some of which reinstituted market and price controls for meat, vegetables and some industrial raw materials in an effort to stabilize urban supplies and prices. These policies were maintained during the deflationary adjustments of 1988 and 1989, aimed at solving the macro-economic problems associated with high inflation and economic overheating. They also reflected the more conservative stance adopted in the wake of the repression of the student movement in June 1989, which again emphasized the primacy of the plan over the market. Nevertheless it was clear, even during 1989, that the market forces developed during the previous ten years could not be halted or reversed. By the end of 1991, therefore, a recovery in agricultural production in 1990-91, especially in grain output, and continued intensification of the free market system led to the reaffirmation of the market orientation of the reforms by the CCP Central Committee, as cited above.

Several points are worth noting about the growth of the free markets between 1978 and 1991 (see Table 1.1 and Figure 1.1). First, the total number of markets more than doubled, growing from 33 300 to 72 759. Second, the number in urban areas grew from zero to just over 13 per cent of the total, indicating the growing role of these markets in urban-rural exchange. Third, the growth in markets experienced two phases of rapid increase, from 1978 to 1980 as the economic pressures of the initial reforms took effect, and from 1983 to 1986 after official policy sanctioned the role of the markets and restrictions on their operation were lifted. The fourth point to note is the large increase in the value of market trade. The Table also shows the values of trade in real terms (deflating by an index of free market prices) and these values are plotted in the chart. The rate of growth was substantial, especially after 1984, and the significance of this market trade can be shown in a number of ways. First, by the end of 1990 urban residents bought some 60-70 per cent of their vegetables and non-staple foods through the free markets, while peasants sold about 50 per cent of their products through them (See *Summary of World Broadcasts*, Part 3, The Far East, FE/W0161/A/2, 9 January 1991). Second, by 1990 roughly one quarter of all retail sales were through the free market compared to one tenth in 1979 (See *Jingji Cankao Bao*, 14 Febuary 1991, p. 2). Third, free market sales of agricultural products in 1989 as a percentage of output are shown in Table 1.2.

The final point to consider is the changing structure of free market trade. With the exception of fodder and farm tools which only increased by around 100 per cent, all of the categories in Table 1.1 experienced large growth in the value traded between 1978 and 1990, many growing by several hundred per cent. Even the grain market, which remains relatively controlled, grew substantially. Furthermore, given the difficulties of compiling statistics on free market exchange, these official figures are likely to understate the actual volume of sales taking place.

As noted above, one of the striking features of this market growth was that it rapidly challenged the early official view that the markets were simply a mechanism for small-scale, local interchange among the peasants. As the markets developed, their nature quickly changed. Already by 1982 it was estimated that in large and medium cities some 70-90 per cent of goods traded in free markets were being resold by traders after having been purchased elsewhere. For small cities and rural areas the estimates were 50-60 per cent and 20-30 per cent respectively (Zhongguo Jingji Nianjian Bianji Weiyuanhui, 1983, p. IV-129). The markets were thus no longer simply places where the peasants exchanged surplus production. As discussed in the following section, the emergence of a network of merchants and traders meant that they were changing into a sophisticated hierarchy of rural exchange.

1.3.3 The Growth of Free Wholesale Marketing

The expansion of the free market system at the retail level inevitably generated strong economic pressures for changes in the structure of wholesale trade. The combination of household independence and access to free markets encouraged specialization and the realization of regional comparative advantage. This forced the markets to expand beyond small-scale trade for local consumption. Goods circulating outside of the state system had to be aggregated in producing areas, moved to major transport centres and cities, and disaggregated for selling to consumers. This required the development of wholesale merchants and transporters, who, in turn needed specialized wholesale market sites with proper facilities. Some wholesale markets were established as early as 1980-81 and, after 1983, they entered a period of rapid growth which soon began to attract serious attention from China's economists (see, for example, Liu Xiandao, 1984; Zuo Zhaoyi, 1984; Cai Fang, 1985; Zhang Quanxin, 1986; Zhang Liuzheng, 1985; and Wei Yalin, 1986).

A review of the development of wholesale markets suggests that, until 1986, there was some confusion in the minds of both officials and economists in China over what was taking place. This reflected both the speed of growth and the changing status of many individual markets as they evolved from direct selling by producers to consumers into trade between specialized producers, wholesale merchants and retail merchants. It also reflected the problems of defining a wholesale market. Many markets shared both retail and wholesale functions. In some cases they were resurrections of historical specialized market fairs, with histories of many hundreds of years. The uncertainties of classification meant that aggregate statistics for wholesale market growth inevitably contained much guesswork. Reports in 1984 suggested there were over 300 in urban areas (Jingji Ribao, 11 July 1984). By mid-1986, estimates had risen to over 3 000 specialized markets and some 4 000 traditional specialized fairs (Renmin Ribao, 13 August 1986). The rapid rate at which change was taking place is obvious (Nongcun Fazhan Yanjiusuo, 1985), as is illustrated by the following examples.

In Chongqing the volume of goods handled through the city's eight wholesale markets almost doubled between 1983 and 1984 and grew to account for over 11 per cent of the value of goods handled in the free markets. At the same time, the number of traders involved rose from 50 000 to some 130 000 (*ibid.*, pp. 106-7). All this occured before the reforms of 1985 which transferred even more products to the free markets. At the same time, the wholesale markets began to act as centres for inter-provincial and regional trade, aggregating local products for shipping outside the province and importing products from outside for local consumption.

In 1986, the Beitaipingzhuang Wholesale Market in Beijing, which has since become one of the capital's key vegetable and fruit wholesale markets, handled goods with a transaction value of ¥35 million, a 40 per cent increase over 1985. In the first quarter of 1987, it experienced a further 40 per cent increase over the same period of the previous year (interview with Zhou Wang, manager, 29 April 1987). By the spring of 1987, bananas on the market in Beijing were all supplied through private merchants from the south, who bought from the peasants in Yunnan and Guangxi, shipped them by rail to Beijing and employed people who handled them on the Beijing wholesale market. By 1988, a survey of wholesale marketing in Beijing (Li Ji, 1989) showed that fruit and vegetables entered the Beijing market by two routes: the urban state-run Vegetable Company which accounted for over 70 per cent of supplies by volume and the free market system which accounted for nearly 30 per cent by volume and 40 per cent by value. Furthermore, given that the state supply system was burdened by huge subsidies, the process of expansion of the free market system and decline of the state system was accelerating. Eventually by late 1991, the Beijing authorities abandoned the system of subsidized supply through state channels.

A final example of a different form of wholesale market growth is provided by Xintizhen in Honghu County, Hubei (Liu Xiandao, 1984). This town had a long history as a centre of trade in rural products before 1949. Its location on the Yangzi River and close to the Honghu Lake gives it convenient water transport links and it also stands at the junction of roads to Wuhan and Shashi. Its wholesale market was established in September 1983. Within six months of operation, it had established links with some five provinces. Local fish, lotus root, melons and chillies were exported out of the county by wholesale merchants. In 1983, state commercial departments handled some 335 tonnes of fish, while the free market handled some 1 485 tonnes, of which some 60 per cent was sold in wholesale volumes. Similarly, in 1983, state commerce in Xintizhen handled some 78 tonnes of fruit, but, in its first four months of operation alone, the free wholesale market handled 582 tonnes. This early phase of development typified the dynamics of the situation, with free market prices and profitability driving a process of specialization and the development of local comparative advantage.

As these examples illustrate, the wholesale markets in large urban centres and in county towns were playing different roles, appropriate to their location. The markets in urban centres were concerned with distributing products to urban consumers and acting as centres of exchange in inter-regional trade. By contrast, markets in smaller county trade centres acted as centres of aggregation for local products and as the route for the supply of specialized products from outside.

Developments which illustrate the economic significance of these markets include their extensive geographical reach, the expanding volume and value of goods handled through them, and the fact that they sometimes trade in 'forward' sales rather than in actual goods. In other words, they have begun to take on the characteristics of wholesale markets in free market economies. This in turn is having knock-on effects on other sectors such as transport, banking and credit, storage, packing, processing, and other forms of market services. Inevitably, such changes have fundamental implications for the behaviour of producers, for the nature of urban-rural exchange and for the way the economy functions. While a proportion of trade in agricultural products is still handled through the state supply and marketing system, it is diminishing. In many major cities, the vegetables, meat, fruit, eggs and other foodstuffs handled through the free markets now typically account for 50-100 per cent of urban consumption. Prices tend to reflect supply and demand and product quality, though in many markets local governments attempt to set upper and lower limits and to control speculation. In addition, it is argued that state commercial agencies should play a role as market stabilizers, buying stocks when supplies are plentiful in order to maintain prices and selling when supplies are short in order to keep prices down (Mao Yufei, 1986).

One final example which illustrates the continuing expansion of the free wholesale markets is the extent to which wholesale grain markets are also beginning to emerge, even though most urban rations are still supplied through the state system at subsidized prices. In 1986 and 1987, reports began to appear in the press that some of the traditional grain market centres were reappearing (Renmin Ribao, 25 November 1986, p. 2 and Xinhua Ribao, 2 January 1987, p. 1). While the amount handled by these markets was insignificant compared to the volumes passing through the state system, they indicated the potential for the emergence of an independent grain marketing network. Nevertheless, the continued existence of state controls over grain and the reassertion of state intervention with the poor harvests after 1985 meant that this trade remained limited (Wu Shuo and Yang Min, 1991). The improvements in grain output in 1990 and 1991, and the continued problems of the costs of state subsidies to both producers and consumers led, however, to a new surge of interest in reforming the grain production and marketing system. More free wholesale markets were established such as those in Jiujiang (Xinxi Shibao, 22 December 1990, p. 1) and Zhengzhou (Zhongguo Shangbao, 8 January 1991, p. 1). Many local experiments to reduce state intervention in the marketing and supply system were begun (Du Ying *et al.*, 1989, and Guo Shutian, 1991). Eventually in late 1991, Vice-Premier Tian Jiyun announced that 'the reform of grain-related operations should aim at commercializing grains and gearing operations to market demands. Once (Zhengzhou's) grain wholesale market becomes fully-fledged, it will become a powerful force to stimulate Henan's economy, and set an example for other grain wholesale markets across the country to model upon (Xinhua news report, *Summary of World Broadcasts*, Part 3, The Far East, FE/1236/B2/2, 22 November 1991). As these developments were occurring, grain prices to consumers were increased, and there was thus a consistent policy orientation towards the development of free market forces in the circulation of one of the most basic of China's agricultural products.

In sum, since 1978, the evolution of free markets in agricultural commodities in China has shown a consistent and accelerating trend towards the use of the market mechanism to regulate production, set prices and structure urban-rural exchange. As the foregoing discussion has illustrated, this process has been characterized by fluctuations in the rate of change and by periods of hesitation and even reversal. In part, this reflected problems of macro-economic adjustment necessary to control inflation and stabilize the changes taking place. In part it also reflected the political complexity of developments which undermined the orthodox approach to production and marketing of the preceding thirty years, changed the distribution of economic powers, and affected the economic relationship between town and countryside. Nevertheless, once set in train, the growth of market forces in China has proved to be a powerful engine of economic change.

1. 4 Price Reform

1.4.1 State Procurement Systems

Until 1979, agricultural prices were exclusively dominated by the state-controlled system of unified purchase and sales. The communes were assigned sown-acreage quotas for major crops and sales quotas for which they were paid state-determined purchase prices. The stated goals of this system were to ensure the supply of essential food and economic crops to urban areas, to promote local self-sufficiency in grain, to increase agricultural prices gradually in order to reduce the "price scissors" between agricultural and industrial prices, and to improve the lot of the peasants. In practice, however, the rigidities of the sown-acreage quotas and of the price system served to undermine all these goals. Supplies to urban areas had to be supplemented by substantial imports of grain and cotton. Local self-sufficiency was bought at a cost in terms of local specialization and peasant incomes (Lardy, 1983). The nominal improvement in agricultural prices disguised the differences in sectoral productivity, the growth in agricultural costs, and other indirect transfers to the urban sector. In a situation of static prices and growing costs, the burdens of the peasants were increasing (for a discussion of the price effects see Sheng Yuming, 1991).

State procurement of agricultural products operated through three types of purchase systems used for the three categories of products (Ma Hong, 1982, pp. 482-509 and Donnithorne, 1967, pp. 337-64). Unified purchase *(tonggou)*, which was used for the first category of goods considered vital for the economy as a whole, was introduced in 1953. The state thereafter monopolized the purchase and sale of these products at prices it determined. Production was carried out according to the sown-acreage plan and producers were given targets for the volume, quality and variety of sales, the ratio between sales and retention for own consumption, and the dates for delivery. The basic sales quota was paid for at the base price and surplus sales were usually rewarded with a percentage loading on top of the base price. Initially the state purchase price for grain was well below the selling price to urban consumers. By the mid-1960s, however, purchase prices had risen above selling prices and the state was thereafter subsidizing the urban areas.

The second type of purchase system was that of assigned purchase *(paigou)*. It was introduced in 1955 and extended in 1959 to cover the market in animal products, important subsidiary foods and some economic crops, most of them being industrial raw materials considered important for the national economy. The state assigned sales targets to producers, and these were embodied in sales contracts between producers and commercial departments based on state-determined prices. In general, the assigned purchase system operated as an extension of the unified purchase system, and until the late 1970s, the two of them accounted for the bulk of all agricultural product purchases by the state.

The third type of purchase system used in respect of all other goods was that of negotiated purchase *(yigou)* whereby commercial departments and producers negotiated contract sales according to demand at mutually agreed prices. Commercial regulations demanded that these prices had to be close to state posted prices and lower than free market prices. The methods for determining negotiated prices was laid down by the State Council. This system was widely used before 1957 but was subsequently abandoned. During the Cultural Revolution goods in this category were handled through assigned purchase. Negotiated purchase was not fully restored until 1979 when it was argued that it should be expanded to cover some 20 per cent of state purchases (Zhang Zhicheng and Wang Qihua, 1979).

In economic terms, there was little difference between these pricing systems. Prices were administratively determined. Producers' sales quotas were fixed. State purchase prices and state selling prices bore little relationship to each other. Prices were irrelevant to distribution, since commodities were allocated in a planned way through the administrative system. Finally, prices did not affect consumer behaviour, since supplies of key commodities were sold by allocated rations.

Taken together, these three purchasing methods accounted for the bulk of trade in agricultural products. Demand came from government and commercial departments through the chain of administrative command to the collective units. The movement of agricultural goods was therefore bound to the territorial framework of administrative control, and marketing links across administrative boundaries were hindered. Prices were generally below free market levels, and in any event as shown above, with the exception of small-scale local exchanges, free markets were severely restricted for most of the period from 1966 to 1978.

1.4.2 The Liberalization of the State Procurement System

The purchasing and price reforms introduced in early 1979 affected this pricing structure in three key ways. The most immediate was the increase in purchase prices and in the price loading for surplus sales. The second way was the liberalization of state procurement systems by relaxing some controls and allowing greater flexibility in the treatment of different categories of goods. The third way, as has been shown, was the re-invigoration of the free markets. The impact of each of these reforms intensified as the household farming system evolved. While they did not immediately change the dominant position of the state purchasing system, they set in motion the forces which began to weaken it. In this section we discuss the liberalization of state procurement and in the following section we look at the process of price reform.

The liberalization of the procurement systems involved a progressive reduction in the base targets for unified sales, the restoration of negotiated sales, and greater freedom to sell the surplus production of unified and assigned category goods at negotiated prices or on the free market. In response, producers attempted to sell a greater proportion of their output in the higher-priced categories or on the free market, and local authorities came under pressure to interpret the rules more liberally or to pay additional local loadings for extra sales. The effect was first to place strains on the state budget which was faced with higher expenditure for agricultural purchases and, thereby, higher subsidies to urban consumers, and second to weaken the state controls over the purchasing system as a whole.

The reduction in base figure targets for sales to the state and the greater flexibility in the application of categories meant that a growing proportion of purchases were made at surplus prices or as negotiated sales. As a result the total value of agricultural product purchases went up. The gross value of agricultural output grew by 5.6 per cent per year for the period 1979 to 1981, for example, while the total value of agricultural purchases went up by 19.6 per year (Lu Baifu and Yuan Zhenyu, 1983). This ensured greater supplies to urban areas, but it also meant that the subsidy costs to the state grew dramatically. For nine commodities including grain, cotton, vegetable oils and meat, the increase in price subsidies from 1979 to 1981 was of the order of 300 per cent. The effect over this period is demonstrated by the declining proportion of state purchases at base prices and by the failure to meet state base-price purchase targets. This reflected both the increased difficulties of enforcing the unified purchase system at the household level and the efforts by producers to shift their sales to higher-price categories. Some peasants, for example, deliberately failed to meet their sales targets and instead sold their grain through a neighbour so that they could get the surplus price. Other peasants sold grain they had obtained from the state at base prices as an incentive to produce meat and other economic crops back to the state at negotiated prices, making a profit on the price differentials *(ibid.)*. There was thus conflict between the maintenance of unified purchasing arrangements, the complexities of a multi-tiered price structure, and the growing possibilities for producers to market their products through different avenues.

Associated problems were caused by the rehabilitation and expansion of negotiated purchases. By 1982, the value of negotiated purchases had risen to 12 500 million yuan and accounted for 11.5 per cent of state purchases (SSB, 1983, p. 388). Apart from the slippage of planned-purchase goods into this category, there was also a loss of control of negotiated prices. Local departments competed to buy products and raised purchase prices independently or offered additional surplus price loadings (Zhongguo Nongye Nianjian Bianji Weiyuanhui, 1983, p. 380). One cause of this development was the growing trend for peasants to sell subsidiary products on the free market or to local processing units rather than to state purchasers. This led to competition among state purchasers and consequent price rises. According to one report, for example, in 1980 there was a 50 per cent increase in the amount of tea retained by collectives to sell themselves. At the same time state enterprises in some areas found that they could not buy enough raw materials for processing. In 1979 and 1980, Shanghai experienced shortfalls in such things as cotton, tobacco, wool, oxhides, raw lacquer, tong oil, feathers and other products. As a result in some areas the purchase prices for 16 out of 40 products in the first and second categories were higher than state posted prices (Shang Zhengyuan, 1982). Eventually, this competition for supplies of commodities led to an explosion of 'commodity wars' and to a dramatic rise in raw material prices which lasted until the economic downturn of 1989-90 (see, for example, Watson *et al.*, 1989).

The examples quoted above should not be exaggerated to imply a complete loss of purchasing and price controls by the state, and it should be borne in mind that in 1982 over 78 per cent of purchases still occurred within the state base and surplus price framework. Nevertheless the growing problems reflected the difficulties of attempting to retain a complex structure of state purchasing while making greater use of price and market incentives. Inevitably this led to many proposals for stricter management of the purchasing system, thereby raising the possibility of a retreat from the trend to use price incentives and markets back to reliance on state quota controls (see, for example, Shang Zhengyuan, 1982 and Lu Baifu and Yuan Zhenyu, 1983). This tendency became particularly evident in the reassertion of controls in the grain and pork markets after 1986 and the concerns with the inflationary explosion of 1988. Such reassertion, however, did not remove the secondary markets. The power to regain control was thus becoming steadily weaker because of the decline of the communes and the expansion of household farming. This multiplied the difficulties of enforcing the planned quota system. In effect, the state authorities faced a choice between following the reforms they had introduced to their logical conclusion, or attempting to stem the tide by reintroducing regulations which could achieve greater state control only at the cost of curtailing the new buoyancy in rural production and conflicting with the organizational reforms also taking place.

Ultimately, therefore, the trend towards liberalization of state procurement and pricing systems was maintained. The total number of agricultural product categories subject to price controls dropped from 111 accounting for 90 per cent of total purchases in 1978 to some 17 accounting for only 30 per cent of purchases in 1987 (interview, Beijing, April, 1989). By 1991, it was estimated that about 50 per cent of all agricultural product purchases took place at market prices, 20 per cent were subject to state guidance prices, where maximum and minimum prices were set, and 30 per cent at state determined prices (Guo Shutian, 1991, p. 18).

1.4.3 Price Increases after 1979

The methods used to determine planned prices for agricultural products has in the past presented Chinese planners with many theoretical and practical problems (Zhao Xinghan, 1984 and Donnithorne, 1967, pp. 434-456). The theoretical issues have included such things as whether prices should reflect a Marxist definition of value, whether they should include a profit rate of capital and how that might be determined, whether they should reflect average production costs and conditions or the worst case, and how average profit might be reasonably defined. At a practical level, price determination has required the collection of empirical data on the factors of production for different crops in different regions and the calculation of production costs. Among the more difficult tasks has been deciding the value to be assigned to labour. Given the many imponderables involved in resolving these problems, prices were usually fixed in a fairly pragmatic way. In general price-fixing tended to rely on exisiting relativities, to discount the value of capital inputs, to adopt the average-case cost-level, and to assume that labour was worth 0.80 yuan a day, despite the wide variations in actual payments to peasants.

Using this approach, over the period from 1958 to 1978 the overall trend in agricultural prices failed to take full account of the increase in agricultural costs. Despite purchase price increases for grains in 1961 and 1966, together with surplus loadings for the periods 1960-61, 1965 and 1971 onwards, and further price adjustments for other products, costs climbed as a proportion of output value and the returns to producers diminished (Su Xing, 1979 and Wu Shuo, 1980).

The price increases begun quietly in 1978 and introduced with much greater fanfare in 1979 were intended to correct this situation by improving agricultural profitability and raising peasant incomes (Lardy, 1983, pp. 88-92). At the same time the increases initiated efforts to use relative prices for different products to influence the internal structure of agricultural production. In addition the prices of some agricultural inputs were reduced so that production costs went down. The prices of cotton, rape seed, animal husbandry products and aquatic products were first raised in 1978. In 1979 the prices of eighteen products were increased an average of 24.8 per cent, including grains (20 per cent rise with a 50 per cent loading for surplus sales), cotton (15 per cent with a 30 per cent loading plus a 5 per cent subsidy for north China), oil crops (25 per cent with a 50 per cent loading) and live pigs (26 per cent). Subsequently further adjustments were made. In 1981 the base price of soyabeans was increased by 50 per cent, bringing it to the previous surplus sales price, while any further loading for surplus sales of beans above the quota was abolished. There were also increases in the prices of cotton, wool, hemp, timber, raw lacquer and tong oil in 1980, and tobacco and vegetables in 1981. Taken as a whole, procurement prices in 1981 were an average of 42 per cent above those of 1977 *(ibid.)*.

Thereafter, the process of price changes reflected the complex interaction between planned prices, market prices and the impact of competition for supplies in the 'commodity wars' mentioned above. In addition, increases in state purchase prices were sometimes accompanied by increases in selling prices and sometimes by the provision of larger subsidies to consumers. State purchase prices therefore became increasingly used as a lever to affect production. Posted prices remained stable during 1982 but there were adjustments in the ratios of purchases at different prices. In 1983 in some parts of north China, for example, cotton was purchased at the ratio of 30 per cent base price and 70 per cent surplus price. In 1984 the ratios became 20 per cent base price and 80 per cent surplus price. In south China there was a ratio of 60 per cent base price and 40 per cent surplus price. In effect this gave a substantial stimulus to the increase of cotton production in the north. As these examples show, the adjustment of prices, both nationally and regionally, was being used to influence production.

By 1984, however, the cumulative effect of such transfers and the strains they imposed on the state budget was leading some economists to argue that the state was not getting enough funds from agriculture (Liang Wensen, interview, 18 January 1984). They felt that the terms of trade had moved too far in favour of agriculture, that some prices should be reduced, and that some of the subsidies for agricultural inputs should be removed. By contrast other economists were more cautious and argued that while some adjustment was needed to change the relative prices for different crops, the state still accumulated a considerable amount from agriculture and it was too early to talk of reducing prices (Zhang Liuzheng, interview, 19 January 1984). These divergent views reflected the new structure of the agricultural economy that was emerging as economists grappled with the problems of using prices and other economic methods of directing production rather than quantity targets. Eventually in 1985, the abolition of the unified purchase system heralded an attempt to fully liberalize the pricing system. In his discussion of the issue at the beginning of 1985, therefore, Zhao Ziyang argued that removing price controls would initially generate price rises but that these would eventually stabilise (Nongmin Ribao, 15 February 1985, p. 1). He cited experiments in vegetable marketing in Guangdong as evidence to support his argument (Zhao Ziyang, 1985).

Unfortunately for Zhao Ziyang and for the optimism surrounding the reforms of 1985, the peasants' response to the price changes initiated a phase of major fluctuations in the output of different commodities and severe food price inflation in cities. The central government chose to re-emphasize price stability and the management of grain, oil and cotton prices, and to relate supplies of base-price inputs to the delivery of base-price sales quotas. At the same time local governments attempted to control the prices of meat and key vegetables. Nevertheless, it was acknowledged that administrative controls could no longer work alone, and price incentives had to be used to encourage producers as well. During 1987 and 1988, plan prices for various products were adjusted upwards (Zhu Min, 1989), and further adjustments were made in 1990 and 1991 (Guo Shutian, 1991). It was therefore not until relative stability of output and prices was achieved again during 1990-91 that price reform once more became an issue of debate (see, for example, Zhong Ming, 1990; Han Zhirong, 1990 and Yang Shengming, 1990), with some economists arguing for greater reliance on planning, some for market forces, and some for various types of balance between them. Eventually the party's decision of late 1991 indicated a return to a continued process of price reform, aiming at an ever-greater role for market prices.

1. 5 Rural Investment

As might be expected the changes in farm management, marketing and pricing discussed above had major implications for the pattern of rural saving and investment (Watson, 1989). Some economists argued that the rapid growth of output in the first half of the 1980s reflected efficiency gains because of the introduction of household farming and that once those gains had been realized, new investment was needed. Others argued that continued high-speed growth could be achieved through further institutional reforms. Such debate, however, had to take account of the new framework for capital accumulation and investment, especially of the enhanced role of the household and the relative decline in the power of government to manage rural saving directly. In the following sections, therefore, we briefly review the management of investment under the commune system, examine the impact of the reforms, and comment on the implications for rural investment.

1.5.1 Saving and Investment under the Communes

From 1958 to 1978 there were four major sources of capital in the Chinese countryside: direct and indirect state investment; collective saving and investment; 'free' labour; and credit. Direct state investment came through state budgetary allocations for agricultural use. Much of this was used for administrative costs, relief and other administrative expenditures, and less than half went to fixed assets and working capital (Lardy, 1983, pp. 133-4). Since much of this went to large-scale irrigation projects and to state farms, the impact on collective farming was limited. Indirect state investment in agriculture consisted of investment in the production of fertilizers, pesticides, agricultural machinery and other farm inputs.

The second source of capital was collective saving through the retention of funds within the communes. This formed the primary source of rural investment. According to one survey, only around 24 per cent of total agricultural investment came from state sources and the rest came from within the collectives themselves (Zhang Liuzheng, 1980, p. 35). These funds were used for investment in both fixed assets and as working capital. The third type of investment, 'free' labour, was also realized within the collectives. It consisted of the use of collective labour for work on infrastructure, land improvement and, especially, water conservation. The labour was 'free' in the sense that it involved the mobilization of peasants during slack agricultural seasons, and the costs were absorbed into the collective work point system (Nickum, 1978).

The remaining source of investment funds for agriculture before 1979 was bank and rural co-operative credit. This was used for both short-term working capital and investment in fixed assets. Although less significant during the Cultural Revolution, bank loans offered an alternative source of capital for collective agriculture.

Overall, therefore, agriculture had to provide the bulk of its investment funds itself and was also used as a source of funds by the state for investment in industry. While this outcome is to be expected in a developing country during the early stages of growth, the evidence suggests that until 1978 the substantial industrial growth which took place in China did not lead to a reduction in accumulation of investment funds from the rural sector.

1.5.2 The Impact of the Reforms on Investment

The reforms after 1978 brought major changes to this structure of finance for investment, affecting both the mechanisms for saving and investment and the economic environment for investment choices (Tam, 1988; Watson, 1989; and Sicular, 1990). Decisions on saving, consumption and investment were decentralized to the household level. The government reduced its direct investment. Local government was given greater flexibility over investment decisions, and larger freedoms were introduced into the credit system. Against that background, changes in both input and product prices transformed the relative profitability of different types of undertakings and encouraged a re-orientation of investment priorities. At the same time, the expansion of the market stimulated diversification of production and created new types of employment opportunities.

Central government investment in agriculture declined from 1978 to 1986, both in absolute terms and as a proportion of expenditure. Contrary to expectations, this decline was accompanied by a similar fall in investment at local levels. Furthermore, with rising costs, the proportion of state expenditure used for productive investment also declined (Feng Guojun, 1987). To some extent, this reduction reflected the fact that the price rises had increased the flow of funds to the rural sector. It was anticipated that private and local investment would take up the slack. The problem was that the gains from the price rises were now going to peasant families rather than to collectives. The amount of capital available to each household was limited, and the choice of its use was based on household preferences. Similarly, greater financial independence given to local government meant that it also gained control over the use of local capital.

The fall in state investment in agriculture was paralleled by an equally abrupt reduction in collective investment. This began even before the communes disappeared, since the introduction of household farming meant that a growing proportion of rural output belonged to the contracting households and collective assets were distributed among them. Inevitably, such changes also meant the disappearance of 'free' labour, since households now had to be paid for any work performed.

Against this background, the role of credit in rural accumulation grew significantly (Tam, 1988). Rural savings and lendings both increased at a time when budget investment was declining, and this greatly enhanced the importance of credit in rural investment. One study concluded that by 1983 producers' own capital accounted for 41.7 per cent of agricultural investment, budget outlays for 8.2 per cent, and credit for 51.1 per cent (Huang Xiyuan *et al.*, 1985). Such estimates demonstrate the growing significance of credit since the reforms began. They also imply a much greater sensitivity to interest rates. Furthermore, this change was accompanied by a growth of cash-in-hand among peasants and the re-emergence of many forms of private money-lending with high interest rates.

In sum, therefore, the impact of the reforms was to reduce state and collective investment, to transfer most agricultural investment decisions to the household level, and to increase the importance of credit as a source of rural investment funds. As discussed in the following section, this transformation also contributed to further changes in the way capital is used in the Chinese countryside.

1.5.3 The Forces Shaping Rural Investment since 1984

Since the early 1980s, the key factors influencing the choices made in rural investment have been: price relativities, household decisions, and government policy. Price relativities determine the relative profitability of different activities and thereby influence producers' decisions. Household choices balance profitability and risk, saving and consumption, and work and leisure. Government policy, by changing such things as prices, subsidies and credit supply, can generate major shifts in the economic environment for investment.

The structure of prices in the Chinese countryside is such that crop farming and grain production are the least profitable and commerce, services, and industry are the most. One survey in 1984 found that in 1984 the net income per mu for grain crops was ¥85 and for economic crops, ¥172 (Rural Economy Survey Group, 1986). These returns were reduced after 1984, when the input costs increased considerably, while purchase prices for grains other economic crops have remained fairly static. By 1987, therefore, some agricultural economists were arguing that problems in grain production were caused by the fact that grain prices were too low, input costs too high and no profit could be earned (Zou Shulin, 1987). These variations in agricultural profitability were reinforced by the variations in the return to labour for different types of work. The same 1984 survey found that the gross return per unit of labour input was ¥4.9 for crop farming, ¥4.4 for animal husbandry, ¥8.4 for processing of agricultural products, ¥8.6 for commerce and catering, and ¥15 for transport and industrial processing. Such differences in returns to labour provided a strong incentive for peasants shift their labour to non-agricultural activities. Furthermore, the differences in returns to labour were also paralleled by differences in the returns to capital. One State Statistical Bureau survey in 1989 found that the net returns per yuan invested were ¥1.83 in the primary sector, ¥2.71 in the secondary sector and ¥14.58 in the tertiary (Yin Sanqiang, 1990). Small wonder, then, that the 1980s saw a substantial shift in private and public investment to non-agricultural activities, particularly towards rural enterprises, and a decline in investment in pure agriculture.

The other major constraint on agricultural investment at the household level is the nature of the land contracts. The scale of the land farmed by each family is very small and cannot absorb much investment in the form of large inputs. Second, despite official reassurances that land contracts will remain stable and can be inherited or sub-contracted to others, peasants remain worried about the long-term future of the land currently under their control. They are not sure who will be the beneficiaries of any investments they might make. Third, all peasants regard the land as the most basic form of economic security. They are unwilling to lease out their small share to others, but lack the incentive to invest in it beyond maintaining existing production. By mid-1987, therefore, as much as 5 per cent of arable land was estimated as being neglected by the households which had contracted it (interview, Beijing, 17 April 1987). The net effect of all these factors was to discourage investment in land, especially in the more developed regions.

Two main conclusions can be drawn from these developments. First, capital at township (formerly commune), village (formerly brigade) and household levels has moved out of agriculture and into rural industry, processing, transport and commerce. These are the most dynamic sectors of the rural economy and generate the highest returns. Second, the household now plays a key role in agricultural investment. Households control the use of land, labour and agricultural output and, with the exception of land, also own most agricultural fixed assets. While government and village decisions can influence the way households use these resources, peasant households will also take into account the opportunity costs involved.

Ultimately, the Chinese government responded to this situation the late 1980s by increasing the amount of direct state investment in agriculture (Sicular, 1990, p. 22). Nevertheless, discussion among Chinese economists indicated that there was continued disagreement over the priorities to be given to different types of investment and over the policies and mechanisms to be used (Lan Gengyun, 1991). Some stressed giving priority to crop farming, while others preferred a continued shift to diversification and non-agricultural enteprises. Some stressed monetary inputs, while others looked for more human capital and scientific development. Some called for an increase in agricultural investment as a proportion of all investment, while others saw an absolute increase but a relative decline as part of the process of economic growth. There was also debate over the different roles of the household, the village and the government, and there were calls for further reforms to the operation of banks and credit systems. In effect, while the momentum established by the reforms was continuing, investment flows were still dominated by the structure of relative prices and profitability.

The above discussion has outlined three major factors (prices, household behaviour and government policy) which now affect the way investment is made in the countryside. In general, they are all tending to work against purely agricultural investment. Furthermore, they operate in an environment where the choices for investment are much wider than before, and where market forces are having a strong impact at the margin. This combination of changes in the mechanisms for accumulation and investment and in the factors affecting investment choices has thus contributed to the dramatic growth of non-agricultural enteprises in the Chinese countryside and to fundamental changes in the structure of the rural economy, as discussed in the following section.

1. 6 Non-agricultural Rural Enterprises

In the context of the decentralization of production management, liberalization of markets and investment environment discussed above, the rapid growth of non-agricultural enterprises in the countryside was almost inevitable. Labour freed from agriculture was available to develop new types of production, spurred on by the higher returns to be gained from such investments. Commonly known as township enterprises, China's rural enterprises are economic units established by local government in the countryside or by the peasants themselves. They encompass all types of economic activity, including agriculture, industry, construction, transport, commerce and services (Chen, Watson and Findlay, 1991).

Rural enterprises operate outside the state plan and are subject to 'hard budget constraints' in that their owners (the peasants or the townships) do not have any guaranteed budget support from above. They buy inputs and sell outputs in free markets and do not have to fulfil plan obligations to the state. Despite this market orientation, however, their origins in the collective system mean that they commonly have a strong linkage with local governments. Rural enterprises can form an important source of local revenue. They can also develop close relationships with other local and regional government-owned industries, acting as processors and sub-contractors and enabling the regional economy to take advantage of the labour and other resources within its administrative area. As a result, local government is keen to promote their growth. It will tend to protect such enterprises and to ensure that they have priority in the distribution of local raw materials, at times intervening in market flows to outside areas.

After 1978, township enterprises experienced an unprecedented phase of rapid development (State Council Research Unit Rural Economy Group and the Rural Development Research Institute of the Chinese Academy of Social Sciences, eds, 1990; see also Chen, Watson and Findlay, [1991] and Findlay and Watson, [1991] for data). The total number of enterprises increased from 1.4 million in 1980 to 18.7 million in 1989, more than a tenfold increase. Their total labour force rose from 30.0 million to 93.7 million, an increase of over 60 million over 10 years, and their total value added increased by a factor of 5. There was a slow-down in growth in 1989, caused by the credit squeeze of late 1988 and the deflationary policies followed in 1989. During 1990 and 1991, however, these policies were relaxed and the growth trends of previous years reasserted themselves.

Value added in rural industry was increasing by about 17 per cent a year (9 per cent a year in real terms) over the 1980s. By contrast, Chen, Watson and Findlay (1991) report that profits and taxes in state-run enterprises increased nearly 2 times between 1980 and 1989, an average growth rate of about 8 per cent (omitting 1989, the average growth rate rises to 9 per cent), their wage bill grew at 13 per cent a year (to 1987) and value added grew at 9 per cent a year (about 5 per cent in real terms). Thus value added in township and village enterprises was growing over the 1980s about twice as fast as that in state enterprises. It accounted for 29 per cent of that in state enterprises in 1984 but rose to 36 per cent in 1987.

As a result of this phenominal growth, by 1990, the total output value of these enterprises accounted for over 54 per cent of rural output value (*Summary of World Broadcasts*, Part 3, The Far East, FE/1005/C1/2, 25 February 1991) and around one quarter of national output value. Their export earnings also made up some 25 per cent of the national total (*Summary of World Broadcasts*, Part 3, The Far East, FE/W0159/A/1, 19 December 1990. See also *Zhongguo Xiangzhen Qiye Bao*, 12 December 1990, p. 3). The national figures, however, disguised significant regional variations (Findlay and Watson, 1991). The growth in the share of rural industries in output was particularly marked in the coastal provinces with low per capita land ratios, dense populations, better infrastructure and the potential for rural enterprises to build profitable links with existing industries.

In sum, the growth of rural enterprises signalled a shift in the nature of China's rural development strategy from an emphasis on crop farming and basic agriculture to reliance on the comprehensive development of agriculture, industry and commerce. This shift was spelt out in the party's report of March 1984 (CCP Central Committee, 1984), which envisaged that the rural enterprises would become the focus of a new phase of integrated rural development, providing inputs for agriculture, absorbing rural labour, helping to raise rural incomes and producing for the market. The development of rural enterprises thus demonstrates that China's rural reforms involved a fundamental shift in the overall approach to rural development.

1. 7 Conclusion

The major themes considered in this chapter were the reintroduction of household farming and free markets in the Chinese countryside, and the implications of these changes for rural investment and non-agricultural enterprises. Our analysis of the evolution of household farming and the free retail and wholesale markets has demonstrated how each phase of economic development after the original changes of 1978 created strong pressures for further reform. What started out as a reform of the system of labour management and of agricultural prices led to the collapse of collective farming as managerial decisions were decentralized to the household. This, in turn, stimulated the growth of free markets which challenged both the state price structure and state controls over the distribution of agricultural products. The influence of the free markets fed back into production by encouraging specialization and forward into distribution by generating wholesale trade. This also began to affect urban-rural exchange. The economic forces generated in this way then proceeded to change the structure of rural investment and led to a new phase of rural economic growth based on the development of rural enterprises. The process of agricultural reform thus developed according to its own economic logic and could not be kept within discrete areas.

Such changes heralded a change in China's rural development strategy away from the former preoccupation with pure agriculture and local self-sufficiency towards a diversification of production based on regional comparative advantage and an integrated approach, involving all sectors and relying on the market as a resource allocation mechanism. Needless to say, this has entailed major political and institutional adjustments. The subordination of economic activity to governmental administration has begun to give way to a pattern where economic linkages no longer coincide with the pattern of administrative control. The bureaucratic system is thereby losing its ability to play a direct role in controlling economic flows. Inevitably, this is a political issue. While administrative obstacles to economic movement across boundaries remain and while local officials remain unwilling to relinquish all of their economic powers (or retain those powers disguised as new forms of ownership, licensing and taxation), the free market system is not yet fully free to follow its own logic of development.

In effect, both the party and government hierarchies have to change their structures and adjust to using indirect methods of influencing market systems without preventing the markets from performing the functions now required of them. As we argue below, where the markets began both to challenge the economic and political authority of the party, the authorities have felt compelled to reassert greater administrative controls.

Table 1.1. **The Growth of the Free Market System, 1978-90**

Item	1978	1979	1980	1981	1982	1983	1984	1985	1986	1987	1988	1989	1990
1) Number													
of markets	33 302	38 993	40 809	43 013	44 775	48 003	56 500	61 337	67 610	69 683	71 359	72 130	72 759
(1) Urban	0	2 226	2 919	3 298	3 591	4 488	6 144	8 013	9 701	10 908	12 181	13 111	13 106
(2) Rural	33 302	36 767	37 890	39 715	41 184	43 515	50 356	53 324	57 909	58 775	59 178	59 019	59 473
2) Value of trade (100 million)													
Nominal	125	183	235	287	333.1	385.8	456.9	632.3	906.5	1 157	1 621.3	1 973.6	2 168.2
Real (1978 $)	125	193	241	276	310	345	408	483	642	708	752	838	
(1) Urban		12	24	34	45.2	55.9	75.2	120.7	244.4	347.1	545.3	723.6	837.8
(2) Rural	125	171	211	253	287.9	329.9	381.7	511.6	662.1	810.8	1 076	1 250	1 330.4
of which:													
Grain and edible oils	20.1	28.6	34.4	36.4	39.4	43.4	45.6	49.6	71.2	84.7	108.1	142.7	146.8
Meat, poultry & eggs	21.2	33.3	42.1	60.9	57.6	72.9	91.8	140.1	246.8	320.3	460	570.6	618.8
Aquatic products	5.2	6.6	9.3	12.1	14.8	18.8	24.1	33.2	64.4	85.4	123	158	182.4
Vegetables	14.3	17.1	21.5	25.5	27.2	33.1	38.3	48.8	96.9	131.1	193	238.2	264.2
Dried & fresh fruits	4	6	7.5	8.8	10.3	13.3	18.6	25.5	59.3	83.1	122.9	161	183.5
Fodder & farm food	10.4	11.5	7.1	8.4	10.5	11.7	13.1	13.9	15.2	15.8	18.3	22.2	23
Large animals	20.9	29.8	26.5	38.9	45.4	41.6	35.6	32.6	31.1	32.6	38.2	38.9	38.3

Sources: Watson (1988) and *Zhongguo Tongjl Zhaiyao* (1991), p. 94.

Table 1.2. **Share of Output Sold in Free Markets, 1989**
(per cent)

Pork	43
Eggs	51
Vegetables	58
Beef	68
Poultry	70
Aquatic products	77
Fruits	80

Source: calculated from *Renmin Ribao*, overseas edition, 29 September 1990, p. 2.

Figure 1.1. **Growth of Markets and Transaction Value, 1978-1990**

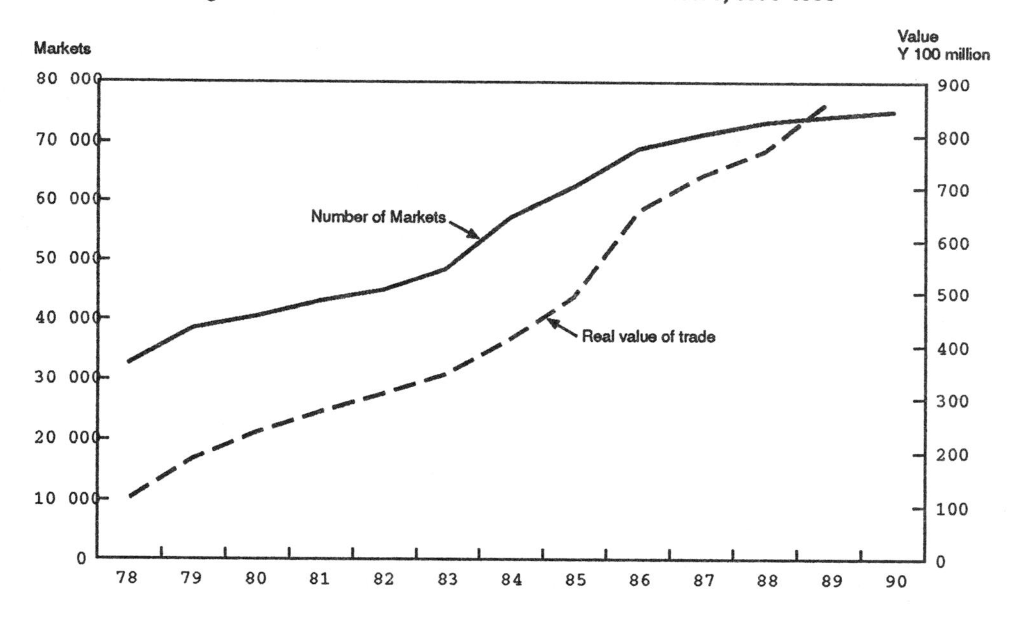

Chapter 2

Policy Issues in the Reform Process

2.1 Introduction

In this chapter we review the experience of particular agricultural sectors of China. The chapter aims to extend the discussion in Chapter 1 by drawing out some themes of the reform process. Rather than discussing each sector in detail and then identifying some themes at the end, this chapter is organised under the headings of the various themes which are illustrated by reference to boxed examples of the experience of particular sectors. In addition, we discuss in some detail some economy-wide policy issues. These include the impact of the management of the international trade system and the impact of the management of macroeconomic policy on agriculture.

The chapter begins with a review of some current issues in agricultural reform in China. Issues associated with pricing policy were discussed in the previous chapter. The focus in this chapter is on institutional issues such as land tenure and farm size. This discussion is introduced by reviewing the literature on the sources of agricultural productivity growth in the 1980s, and, in particular, the sources of the slowdown in agricultural output after 1985.

This discussion and some of the intersectoral issues which are raised here lead into a discussion in the final section of the chapter of some issues which are amenable to quantitative analysis and which are considered in later chapters.

2.2 Sources of Agricultural Productivity Growth

Following the reforms of 1978, growth rates of agricultural products increased across the board. Previously high growth had been achieved in some sectors but only at the expense of others. A side effect of this rapid output growth was that for a short while in the mid-1980s, China became a net grain exporter. But this situation was not continued and net imports returned in 1987 and thereafter. Indeed, the growth of output of grain, and cotton as well, slumped after 1984 (see Box 2.1).

Box 2.1 Grain and Cotton Output Growth Slumps after 1984

The table below shows the average annual growth rates of output of selected agricultural products over the 1980s. The period 1978 to 1984 was remarkable for the high growth rates achieved across the board. But after 1984, up to 1987, the output of grain stagnated and the output of cotton declined. Also the growth rate of oilcrops output nearly halved, although remaining high in absolute value. The other products in the Table however generally retained the growth rates of the period before 1984. So, apart from cotton, there was an impressive growth of farm products other than grain in the second half of the 1980s. Then in the last few years of the decade, shown in the third column, the growth rates of grain and cotton recovered. However much of the growth in this period occurred just in the last year, 1990.

Annual Growth Rates of Output of Selected Agricultural Products (per cent)

	1978-1984	1984-1987	1987-1990
Grain	4.3	-0.7	2.4
Cotton	19.3	-9.8	0.8
Oilcrops	13.8	8.3	0.0
Sugarcane	11.0	5.6	5.9
Sugarbeet	20.5	11.5	4.6
Milk	17.8	12.7	7.3
Red meat	10.3	9.2	7.5
Tea	7.5	7.1	1.9
Fish	4.8	14.4	8.2
Fruit	6.9	14.1	3.7
Tobacco	6.3	11.2	7.7

Source: China Statistical Yearbook, various issues

Lin (1989) divides the sources of growth in agricultural output over these two periods into three components: the volume of inputs, the productivity with which those inputs are used, and an unexplained residual. Lin's results are summarised in Table 2.1. In the first period of 1978-1984, labour and capital made positive contributions to input growth but the most important contributor on the input side to the growth in output was fertiliser (which accounted for about 60 per cent of the growth in inputs). Contributors to the growth in productivity were the price reforms, in conjunction with the household responsibility system and the increased scope for regional specialisation. Lin divided the contributors to productivity growth into those related to the household responsibility system and those related to price and other market reforms. He attributed over 90 per cent of the productivity growth up to 1984 to the introduction of the household responsibility system. In a study using a similar methodology but applied to the period 1978-1984, McMillan, Whalley and Zhu (1989) found that about 80 per cent of the increase in input productivity in agriculture was due to institutional change and the rest to the price reforms. They stress that according to their results the important source of productivity growth in this period was changes in the system of making payments to producers rather than price increases. However prices, especially following the marketing reforms, will continue to have important effects on the mix of agricultural output, as we discuss below.

After 1984, the introduction of the household responsibility system was completed so there was no scope for it to make a further contribution to productivity growth. But price changes and the scope for regional specialisation continued to make a contribution, according to Lin's analysis. In this period, the growth rate of input of chemical fertiliser declined. The estimate of the size of farm labour input fell, according to Lin's estimates, from its peak level in 1984, and fell even faster in the crop sector to which Lin's analysis applies. All these factors contributed to the slow-down in growth.

Another study of these issues but limited to the period up to 1985 is reported by Fan (1991). Fan attempts to separate out the contributions of technological change and institutional reform (via its effects on efficiency improvement) on output growth. He reports that over the 20-year period, about 58 per cent of output growth was due to growth of inputs and 42 per cent was due to productivity improvements. Of the latter, about 27 points was attributed to the efficiency gains from institutional change and 15 points to technological change. The latter share, Fan argues is relatively small. Fan also stresses that the sources of growth vary significantly between regions of China. He reports that the contribution of traditional inputs like land, labour, and manurial fertiliser has been falling rapidly. What he calls modern inputs, such as machinery and chemical fertiliser, have become more important sources of output growth.

The importance of modern inputs is reflected in recent experience. As noted in Box 2.1, there was a resurgence of output growth of grain and cotton in 1990. Grain output grew by more than 6 per cent compared to 1989 and cotton output was nearly 16 per cent higher than in 1989. Higher output in these years was attributed to increased inputs, in particular, larger sown areas, and greater yields. The latter were due to favourable weather, use of fertiliser and in the case of grain, the use of new hybrid seed. It was also expected that the larger output volumes would tend to depress prices and lead to reduced grain and cotton production in the following year.

These results prompt a series of questions about the scope for further productivity growth which we now review. In doing so we also illustrate the nature of these issues by reference to recent events in a variety of agricutural sectors.

2.3 Potential Sources of Further Agricultural Productivity Growth

2.3.1 Extending the Scope of the Market and the Reform Cycle

There is still considerable scope for extending the role of the market in setting prices and allocating supplies of agricultural products. As described in Chapter 1, a large proportion of output of many commodities can already be handled in discretionary (that is, via the market) fashion by producers. Other markets are still largely directed by the state with some scope for market sales of surplus output. Examples are grains, cotton and vegetable oil. Still other products are monopolized by the state, for example tobacco and raw sugar. The reasons for differing degrees of market orientation in each sector is an interesting issue which we address as we proceed through this chapter. While for those products where a large proportion of output is already traded in the market a further increase in that share may have little impact on productivity growth, it is possible that a higher degree of market orientation, in the grain or cotton sector for example, could have a large impact on productivity.

A number of commodities have moved through a series of stages of reform, cycling between control and relaxation. In Chapter 1 we raised the issue of the tension between a market orientation in the allocation of resources and the administrative system. In this chapter we illustrate how this tension is highlighted in these types of reform cycles. Boxes 2.2 and 2.3 report case studies of this process in the grain sector and the pork sector. Some of the common elements in these cycles are:

- the existence of dual marketing systems;
- rapidly growing consumer demand for the product, and urban consumer sensitivity to price changes;
- long production periods, so that output responds to price changes or shifts in incentives with a lag.

To some extent, the nature of these cycles may reflect the experimental and incremental nature of the reforms themselves. The changes set in train by one particular reform may have required further adjustments later on. Furthermore, it is important not to interpret adjustments as necessarily reflecting a rejection of the reforms by some in the Chinese leadership. That may be the case, but it may also be the case that the government has to take action to, for example, control inflation before it can proceed to the next phase of reform. In other words, as shown in Chapter 1, these cycles have occurred around a consistent and general trend.

In practical terms, such a process might arise as follows. The increased overall degree of autonomy accorded to producers as a result of the reforms leads to greater responsiveness to relative price changes. This can then lead to rapid decreases in supply of a particular controlled commodity as producers shift to more profitable crops. Prices for that commodity then rise in free markets and the pressure increases on the state distribution system to guarantee supplies at base prices. Urban consumers put pressure on policy-makers to resolve the 'chaos', and policy-makers respond by suppressing the free market, trying to divert supplies back into the state system.

Some distinction is required at this point between the different groups of policy-makers. The state is unwilling to relinquish all its influence, especially for products about which urban consumers are highly 'price sensitive'. As part of the reform process, however, the centre has passed down responsibility for managing the marketing system to regional governments. The response is generally a 'balkanisation' of agricultural marketing as local governments intervene in trade in local products and in local market supplies. This in turn leads to losses of the gains from regional specialization and trade and to much more unstable markets. The ultimate response may be a reinstatement of central control, only to be followed by another debate about stagnation (see below the discussion about grain problems) and its origins. This might then lead to another burst of reform and, in this way, the cycle can be sustained.

Box 2.2 Grain Marketing Reform

Li Qingzeng (1991) argues that reforms to the grain marketing system in China have followed a series of cycles. The previous state procurement system which had lasted for 30 years was abolished in 1985 (see Chapter 1 above). At that time there were plentiful supplies of grain for two reasons. One was the growth in output after 1978. The other was a rapid increase in imports (averaging nearly 14m tonnes a year between 1978 and 1984 — see below). It appeared therefore that the old problem of a 'grain shortage' had disappeared, so the state procurement system was dismantled. Further evidence of this change was the rapid build-up in stocks of grain in China. Another force for reform was that the commitment of the state to take all the grain that was available at the state-set prices was creating a substantial financial burden.

The state then shifted to a contract system of buying grain, that is, fixed but negotiated quantities, and the contract prices were lower than before. The free market prices for grain also fell as the state tried to clear some of its stocks in 1985. Producers now had greater autonomy and they responded to the relative price changes. As a consequence, grain output fell rapidly. But then market prices started to rise again. The perception among policy-makers was that grain was 'short' once again (imports had also fallen). Their response was a partial return to the old procurement system. Contracts were no longer negotiated and were replaced instead by fixed obligations. Nevertheless, as we noted in Chapter 1, producer response was sluggish and it was not until further price increases were made that production picked up again in 1990-91. By the end of the cycle in 1991, policy-makers were again confidently talking of further marketing and price reforms for grain.

This cycle in reform was made more likely, Li argues, because of the use of a double-track marketing system. Li calls the two components of the marketing system the 'dead' part and the 'live' part. The dead part refers to the grain purchased by the state through contract and mainly supplied to urban residents and industry. The live part refers to grain traded on the free market where its price is set. The argument of the policy-makers was that grain was such a special commodity that at least some grain should be traded through a controlled marketing system, at least in the interim. The long-run ideal was to have the live part take over the dead part. But there were major problems in having the two systems operating side by side. The first was the ever-present incentive to divert supplies from the dead to the live part of the market, thereby encouraging corruption. The other was that as the central government tried to live up to its commitment to reform by reducing the amounts of grain purchased by contract, it was also concerned about the risk of not having access to all the grain required to satisfy urban and industrial demand. It accordingly also passed purchase obligations on to local governments. They were supposed to buy grain according to local market conditions. The local governments then however became concerned about the risks of not meeting their targets, and turned the targets into obligations. Central compulsory procurement of grain was replaced by systems of local compulsory procurement. Peasants tried to evade this new system, and local governments responded by setting up road blocks to try to restrict grain 'exports'. These responses also had the effect of inhibiting innovation in the marketing systems which are be critical if the 'live' part of the system is to take over.

Box 2.3 The Hog Reform Cycle

Sheng *et al.* (1990) identify what they call a hog reform cycle. The system in which the state procured pigs from producers, suppressed all the alternative marketing channels and sold pork to consumers at a low price operated for more than thirty years. While it stabilised the market price, the interests of producers were not given much attention. Producers were always sensitive to relative returns. Even in the state-regulated marketing system, producers were given subsidies and other incentives to increase output, to try to offset the low state procurement prices. After the rural reforms began in 1978 and grain output grew rapidly, the constraint due to feed supplies on pork production was relaxed. Pork output rose rapidly too, in the manner expected from the 'hog cycle'. The margin between the free market price and the state price narrowed as a result.

In early 1985, the government announced the replacement of the compulsory procurement scheme by negotiated purchases. Other subsidies to producers were also rescinded. This increased the degree of household autonomy in pig production, and some households became specialist pig producers. However pig prices stayed low; the peasant's view in the mid-1980s was reported to be that 'raising four legs (pigs) is less profitable than two legs (chickens), raising two legs is less profitable than one leg (mushrooms), and raising one leg is less profitable than no legs (fish)' (*Renmin Ribao*, 11 February 1988).

The reforms occurred at a time when pig prices were low, but this meant that as a result of the greater degree of producer autonomy, the reforms did not lead to a large growth in pig numbers. Nevertheless, the demand for pork was growing rapidly with rising incomes. In 1987, pork 'shortages' started to reappear. Prices in the free market rose again. Consumers went back to the state shops to buy their pork, despite its lower quality than free market pork. This increased the pressure on the state distribution system, which was still operating. Some dealers bought pork from the state shops and resold it on the free market. The rising price of pork led to complaints from the urban residents. As a result, in late 1987, a system of compulsory procurement was reinstated and rationing of pork was introduced in many cities. The new system had similar characteristics to the old one, except that it was now managed by local government, not by the central government.

Why was regulation of the market reintroduced in this case? First, pork price changes had significant effects on the real incomes of urban consumers, because of its budget share. Second, a drop in supply tends to lead to higher prices for longer periods for commodities like pork, which have long growing periods and fewer close substitutes (see the case study of vegetable marketing below for a contrasting example). Furthermore in the Chinese case, pigs were raised on a small scale, and in rural households. Feed quality and genetic characteristics of the animals led to much longer growing periods than in other countries and a very low slaughter rate. Thus the cycles in prices tend to be longer-lasting in China, creating a more significant political problem and therefore more likely to lead to intervention.

The characteristics of pork production suggest that in the face of growing demand for pork, the cycles in production could be matched in the long run by cycles in policy as well. However, the long-run outlook for pork marketing depends on events in the grain market and the availability of grain supplies. There might also be scope to relax the political constraints by transferring to producers new production technologies which reduce the growing periods and raise slaughter rates. However given the growing conditions and the requirements of faster-growing pigs for higher quality grain, the trade-offs would need careful assessment.

2.3.2 Agricultural Product Processing and Internal Trade Barriers

Some agricultural outputs are inputs into the light industrial sector. Cotton and wool are the obvious examples. The growth of rural industry has added to the demand for these fibres. Competition over supplies in a marketing system where there remains a considerable degree of control has led to competition between administrative units using the instruments of regulation, rather than through prices. As discussed above, the result has been the emergence of a series of 'commodity wars' (also see Box 2.2 on the grain war), and in Boxes 2.4 and 2.5 we highlight the experience of the cotton war and the tea war respectively.

The cotton war had its origins in the growth of rural industry to satisfy the growing demand for textiles and clothing in China. As a result of price controls for both outputs and inputs, however, a pricing mechanism was not operating to induce shifts in the supply of and demand for raw cotton. The gap between was resolved instead by the use of other forms of regulation, as local governments attempted to intervene in the inter-regional trade in raw cotton. This time they intervened not to meet their commitments to the central government and to satisfy consumer demands for re-regulation (as in the case of pork and grain), but because of the benefits created for local rural enterprise. Parts of China which were not highly self-sufficient in raw cotton then went back onto world markets for raw cotton. At various times therefore China has been both a significant importer and exporter of cotton. This reflects the domestic price controls, as well as other barriers to internal trade in China.

Exactly the same sort of process occurred in the wool market. The extra dimension in the wool market relates to the lack of variation of wool prices for quality. Local producers have little incentive to grow wool of the types demanded by the processors (this is also an issue in the tea industry — see Box 2.8). The search for high quality raw wool to blend with local products is thus an additional pressure in the case of the wool market for dealing in the international market. Stocks of locally produced wool are high for the same reasons.

The price controls on raw materials, alongside a rapid growth in rural processing capacity, therefore induced a series of commodity wars which were characterised by barriers to inter-regional trade in China. Price reforms for industrial raw materials like cotton and wool would reduce the incentives to impose these barriers, and would lead to patterns of production more likely based on regional comparative advantage. The net effects of these sorts of reforms on China's fibre trade will be to reduce the incentives to divert local supplies onto the world market, and instead lead to increased exports of processed products. Domestic output of fibre could increase, although the size of that increase depends on events in other markets for substitutable outputs.

2.3.3 Marketing Institutions

The discussion below of the shifts in the composition of consumer budgets stresses the rapid growth of non-staple food products. The implication is that to meet the shifts in demand, new marketing arrangements for those products would be required. The changes in the marketing arrangements for fruit and vegetables outlined in Box 2.6 provide a case study of this process.

Box 2.4 The Cotton War

The Chinese textile and clothing industry became China's largest earner of foreign exchange after 1986. From 1987 onwards, however, the industry had difficulty in obtaining sufficient supplies of raw materials. As noted above, China's cotton production reached a peak of 6.3 billion tonnes in 1984 and then declined to 3.5 bt in 1986. By 1990 output was up to 4.5 bt, its highest level since 1984. The degree of utilisation of capacity in the cotton textile industry remained however low through the second half of the 1980s.

Zhang (1991c) identifies a number of factors contributing to these problems. The first was the change in the marketing arrangements for cotton which shifted the relative returns away from cotton towards other crops. Prior to 1985, the state was the only purchaser of cotton. Producers had to meet a basic quota with higher prices offered for over-quota output. There were also other subsidies for inputs, and access to cheap grain in proportion to cotton output. This system was replaced by contract purchases in 1985 but the continuing low contract prices, and the decline in the extent of other subsidies, saw producers switch out of cotton. In reponse to the 'shortage' the government shut down other cotton marketing systems and reinstated state control in 1987.

The low cotton price and accumulation of funds for investment in labour-intensive industry led to large increases in cotton textile-making capacity. Rural enterprises were owned by local governments, as explained in Chapter 1, so those governments took steps to try to guarantee cotton supplies for factories under their control. This led to intervention in the regional trade in cotton, and the development of a cotton war, as governments competed with each other to secure cotton supplies. As output increased, the price of textiles and clothing on the free market fell. Unlike rural enterprises which sold their output on the free market, the state enteprises continued to sell a large part of their output into the state distribution system. Prices there were guaranteed and remained high despite the drop in free market prices.

In period 1984 to 1988 China had remained a net exporter, even over the period of the cotton war. The level of exports was another reflection of the distorted raw cotton price and the incentives to divert supplies onto the world market. Cotton output grew after 1988, and in 1989 and 1990 the government sanctioned large imports of raw cotton, so that in those two years China became a net importer again (0.25 mt in both years). The growth in domestic output and the higher level of imports, combined with the drop in demand for the final products in 1989 and 1990, reduced the intensity of the inter-regional cotton war.

Box 2.5 The Wool War

The problems of sequencing reforms also led to a wool war (see Watson, Findlay and Du, 1989). The demand for wool products had increased rapidly after 1978 as a result of rising domestic incomes and increasing exports of textiles and clothing. The increase in demand for finished products led to a rise in the demand for raw wool as well. Markets for finished products were however relatively more free than markets for raw materials like wool, so finished product prices rose relative to raw wool prices. At the same time, meat markets were being reformed and meat prices were rising, leading to a higher slaughtering of sheep and a lower wool clip than otherwise. The demand for final products, the apparently low price of wool, and the profitability of textile production, supported decisions by regional governments to invest in wool textile production capacity.

The consequent growth in demand for wool fibres put pressure on the state commercial system which at that time still dominated wool marketing. Attempts to by-pass that marketing system emerged and a secondary market for wool also developed. In 1985, the state decided to relax its control over the wool marketing system. The old centralised marketing system was replaced by purchase through contract or through the market. The strong demand for wool was then reflected in market forces and the domestic price boomed.

Access to the international market was restricted by the foreign exchange system which although it permitted considerable import growth, still limited imports below what would otherwise have been observed. There ensued a struggle over the supplies of raw wool. The actors in this struggle included various types of enterprises, both within the plan and outside it, various levels of government, and various types of merchants. In addition, wool growers, who had attained higher levels of responsibility over their clip, became much more sensitive to relative price changes.

The battles over the clip did not solely take the form of competition and rising prices. Regional governments, in pursuit of their perception of local processing interests, raised barriers to the movement of wool within China. These barriers to inter-regional trade, as well as the processing of wool in local mills which could be less efficient than coastal specialists, raised the costs of this fibre war. In addition, even though prices rose, there were few complementary reforms to the marketing system, and over the period of the wool war (1985-88) the quality of the clip actually fell.

The wool war subsided after 1988. The cost of capital to the textile industry to purchase raw materials was by this time very high. The slower growth of the urban economy at the end of the 1980s slowed down the growth in demand for products. By late 1989, textile producers were holding large stocks of finished products. There were also significant stockpiles of raw wool, both in the commercial system and in the hands of growers.

Thus the wool war was not brought to an end by the development of an integrated market along with a restoration of inter-regional trade in wool, but by the slump in demand. There have been some marketing reforms since 1988 (e.g. some wool auctions) but the underlying structure that led to the wool war remains in place. Avoiding another wool war when high growth rates are restored requires a transition to a national market, based on clearly defined wool standards, and on changes in local government behaviour, especially in relation to their incentives to regulate inter-regional trade.

The Box 2.6 is derived from a study by Watson (1991b) which examines the reforms to the vegetable wholesale marketing system in China. He identifies a number of major issues currently facing Chinese policy-makers. These are:

- the conflict between the aim of liberalising fruit and vegetable production and marketing and maintaining low or stable prices.
- the change in the structure of demand for fruit and vegetables, with a shift towards demand for higher quality.
- changes in the structure of production which have resulted in changes in the sources of supply for some urban areas (this has been more marked in some cities, e.g. Beijing, than in others, e.g. Shanghai which has better growing conditions). This in turn has placed new demands on transport, storage and marketing facilities as a whole.
- a proliferation of marketing systems with a growth of free market structures alongside the state system. To some extent, these systems are handling different types of products, with fine vegetables and products from distant areas largely flowing through the free market system. The state system tends to concentrate on the bulk supply of key vegetables by season.
- considerable regional variation in the pattern of the reforms. By and large, southern cities have been more successful in their changes and have gone further than northern cities.
- an emerging sophisticated pattern of inter-regional fruit and vegetable trade which needs much better information, transport, and service facilities.

In essence these problems are associated with a fundamental change in the nature of marketing in China. The system is moving away from a planned model based on local self-sufficiency towards a model based on inter-regional dependency and free market interaction. Aspects of these changes are outlined in Box 2.6.

Overall, the process of change in the past ten years has tended to improve fruit and vegetable production and to introduce much greater variety into urban diets. Compared to the marketing of other products such as grain and pork, the marketing of fruit and vegetables is characterized by relatively low levels of regulation.

2.4 Moving to the Technological Frontier

Researchers in the Chinese Academy of Sciences have identified a number of technological strategies that will contribute to further growth in output (interviews, May 1991):

i) Per unit yield growth is important and, from the CAS perspective, the history of previous increases in yields suggests that further increases are possible. The World Bank argues (1990b) that there is a technology gap in China and that varieties now available in China may have reached the limit on potential increases in yield. Foreign varieties are reported to have yielded in some places 30 to 50 per cent more than Chinese varieties. However the World Bank stresses that barriers to imports of new seed varieties will have to be removed before these sorts of improvements are possible. It is, however, difficult to estimate the likely growth in yields in the long run. Scientists are

Box 2.6 Vegetable Marketing

The process of institutional and managerial change occurring in this transition can be conceptualised in terms of the two models illustrated below:

Schematic Models of Wholesale Market Structures

A. Planned system

Producer (produces according to quota and with subsidies)
↓
Ministry of Commerce (MOC) or Supply and Marketing Co-operative (SMC) (buys by quota, may also do the packing, then delivers by quota)
↓
Urban SMC (MOC delivers to urban SMC which may then sort pack and store)
↓
Local distribution (the urban SMC arranges local distribution)
↓
Consumer

B. Market-type system

Producer (produces for market, stores and packs)
↓
Wholesale market (the producer delivers direct to wholesale or through an agent to wholesale)
↓
Retail
↓
Consumer

China is currently developing free wholesale markets in order to reduce the institutional boundaries between systems operating in the first model, and opening marketing to any participant in order to develop freer vegetable markets. This reflects underlying trend to move from the first model towards the second. Since this transformation also entails a change in the distribution of economic benefits between producers, commercial institutions and consumers, it entails institutional conflicts and requires institutions to be adjusted.

The extent to which the Chinese fruit and marketing system can shift from one model to the other will be constrained by the rate of institutional reform and by the economic and technical constraints on the realisation of a regionally integrated production, supply and marketing system.

It was argued that in the case of pork, for example, the factors contributing to continued intervention, or a cycle of reform and control, included the importance of the commodity in consumer budgets and the length and amplitute of the price cycles. Vegetables as a whole also account for a large share of consumer budgets, but no one item accounts for a large share. That is, there are many substitutes within this category. Given the seasonal variation in supplies, high prices for one commodity will lead consumers to switch into the commodity coming into more plentiful supply. They are therefore less sensititive to changes in any one vegetable price.

The main issues in the vegetable system are at the wholesale level, that is, the need to remove administrative barriers to inter-regional trade. The threat of instabilities in supply has meant that many urban governments have been unwilling to withdraw completely from the vegetable production and marketing systems. It is likely that this situation will continue for some time. Urban governments will however continue to adjust their administrative methods to build more regionally integrated production and marketing systems. They will also be anxious to ensure basic supplies, especially to low-income households. Both targets will more easily be met by easing access to a wide range of possible supplies, that is, by a more extensive set of inter-regional trading arrangements.

reluctant to commit themselves to any particular figure given the uncertainties involved and the difficulties of disentangling the contribution of science from that of other factors.

ii) Another option is to raise the (double) cropping index. At present the national average cropping rate is 112 per cent but in some parts of South China it could rise to as high as 180 per cent. To do that also requires investment.

iii) Targeting potentially high yielding areas is another option. In these high yield areas it is possible to get more than 300 kg per mu (current average yields are about 246 kg per mu). Some experimental fields in South China have produced 1 000 kg per mu.

iv) Solving problems of land degradation is a priority. Land degradation is in many areas caused by the excessive use of chemical fertiliser. As a result the use of fertiliser has been decreased especially in southern China. A related strategy is to use more organic fertiliser and to grow green fertiliser on fallow land. There is 0.53 billion mu of land (out of a total of 1.6 billion mu[1]) which is now classified as 'marginal', of which about 30 per cent could be converted into farm land, but doing so requires a great deal of investment, for example, in irrigation systems. About 50 per cent of arable is currently irrigated.

v) Grain is an input into animal production. At present the protein content of the grain is low so that a greater volume is required for stock feed than would otherwise be the case. Efforts could be made to raise the protein content of maize for example. Breed improvement might also raise the efficiency with which grain is used. Another option is to seek out new sources of food, for example, from tree crops grown on hilly slopes. Examples are walnuts, chestnuts and fruit. The use of hilly land in this way also produces an environmental benefit.

In summary, there is scope for further productivity growth through technological change in Chinese agriculture and many other examples could be given, but in every case, technological change requires an increase in the rate of investment in agriculture.

2.5 Land Tenure and Land Management Reform

As discussed in Chapter 1, a common assessment of the land tenure arrangements in China is that they have adverse incentive effects for investment in agriculture. There are continuing restrictions on rights to transfer land and there is always the threat of administrative intervention in the allocation of land in any area. Farmers will be even less inclined to invest in agriculture in circumstances where the benefits of their investments might be reaped by someone else. This is likely to be the case even if there are reforms to pricing and marketing arrangements which remove the distorted prices faced by many agricultural activities.

Another land management issue relates to economies of scale in the size of farming units. At present, the average area per household is small and, it addition, land allocations are usually fragmented. There are likely to be economies reaped by increasing farm size, if only because of the reduction of the costs of managing multiple plots. There has been a debate in China about the consolidation of land holdings. This debate has been prompted by the stagnation in the growth of grain output, as predicted from our earlier analysis of process of the reform cycle. One argument is that larger farm sizes are required to encourage farm mechanisation, and returning to the collective system is required to achieve larger farm sizes. In the political environment after June 1989, this position was argued forcefully by some, using the idea of economies of scale. However, there are market-type mechanisms which facilitate the use of more mechanised farming methods, for example, contracting out land to more specialised households. The real issue, therefore, is the regulation of these contractual arrangements.

An outstanding example of these issues of ownership and tenure arises in the forestry sector. An outline of the issue in that sector in southern China is presented in Box 2.7.

2.6 Managment of International Trade

2.6.1 Development of Trade

The mangement of trade policy in China has also undergone a substantial set of reforms. Martin (1992) summarises the shifts in China's trade policy over the 1980s. He argues that there were four main changes. First, tariffs were cut in the early 1980s, although not sufficiently to remove the cascading structure of protection in which more highly processed products were protected relative to raw materials. The relative prices within China were therefore altered in favour of processing activities, compared to the production of raw materials.

Second, after 1985, the shift to the agency system, in particular for imports, led to a closer relationship between domestic and international prices of traded manufactured goods (but not raw materials). This meant that the production decisions of enterprises in China were influenced directly by relative prices from world markets.

Third, a system of retention of foreign exchange earnings by producers and lower levels of government was introduced. By the mid-1980s the retention rate was up to about 25 per cent and has since gone higher.

Finally there have been two periods of substantial devaluation, first in 1985/86 then in 1989/90[2]. These substantially cut the over-valuation of the exchange rate, reducing the extent to which exports had to be subsidised from the government's budget. In early 1991, the government announced a plan to remove all remaining direct subsidies for exports. The devaluation also facilitates direct dealing between producers, or trading companies, and the world market.

A consequence has been a rapid increase in the international orientation of the Chinese economy. The sum of exports and imports is now equal to about a quarter of GDP, three times higher than when the reforms began. There has also been a rapid growth in foreign investment in China.

Box 2.7 Timber

Many of the new problems introduced by the reforms have been generated by the nature of household operation and by the impact of the dual price structure on timber producers and markets. Watson (1991a) argues that the main problems are: the wanton felling of trees and the limitations of household management.

Indiscriminate felling of trees has been a long-term problem in China with various periods of development (such as the Great Leap Forward) being associated with extensive cutting. The decentralization of authority to households, the opening up of free markets at higher prices, and the rapid growth in demand has increased the problems. State Council proclamations calling for controls over felling were issued in January 1979 and December 1980. Subsequent laws and documents all stressed the need to control the trend and to establish the principle of limiting removal to or below the growth rate. None have been successful. The current system of issuing felling permits does not work since peasants find ways round the rules and local governments often issue permits indiscriminately.

The limitations of household forestry production include:

- remaining uncertainties over the long-term rights to land and the returns on investment;
- the lack of capital available to households for large and long-term investment;
- the lack of technical and managerial skills;
- the fragmentation of land management presenting problems of co-ordination and planning for species selection, pest control, planting and so forth;
- problems of producing and distributing seedlings;
- the provision of services and the efficient management of felling, transport and marketing.

Furthermore, the general shortage of credit and the rising interests rates make the risks of loans for investment in forestry more expensive. In many ways the technical requirements of forestry, the large investment required, and the slow rate of return, would appear to conflict with the subdivision of land into family blocks. On the other hand, economic and social inequalities might have been created if land had been selectively divided to a smaller number of families capable of managing it at the time of the introduction of the household responsibility system.

In the view of many Chinese observers, the solution to these difficulties should be found through greater integration. Three main types of co-operation have been discussed in Chinese journals. First, co-operation among households through forms of joint management. This is seen as a means of aggregating resources and sharing risks. It involves forms of co-operative management, shareholding and joint distribution of returns. The second involves more unified management by village collectives. Households should have freedom of day-to-day management and obtain direct returns from sales, with the village providing unified direction for planning, input supplies, technical specifications and so forth. The third type involves more direct action by local government, especially at county level. This might include various types of contractual relationships between households and the government, local government investment in seedling farms and other projects, and direct investment by local government. Various model examples of these types of response to the problems have been cited. The authors generally stress that this should not be seen as a reversion to the collective system and that economic efficiency and market operation should still be seen as important. The institutional and managerial framework for forestry in south China will therefore remain in a state of flux, with many different forms of management co-existing.

There remain substantial barriers to trade and distortions in China's international trading system. Quantitative controls on both imports and exports continue. While there has been a boom in the number of foreign trade corporations, they still trade on their own account in export transactions and they fail to pass on world price changes to exporters. Responsibility for these corporations has been decentralised and not all operate under strict hard budget constraints. The foreign exchange system is a major source of distorted signals as we discuss below. Despite these issues, however, the reform of the trading system over the 1980s has been substantial.

An interesting case in which domestic marketing reforms had significant implications for China's trade and the trading institutions is the tea war of 1985 to 1988. This case has been reported in detail by Forster (1991), and is summarised in Box 2.8.

Apart from the increasingly international orientation of the economy, another aspect of those reforms is the evolution of China's pattern of trade. A number of authors (eg. Anderson, 1990; Warr and Zhang, 1990; and Zhang, 1991b) have used indicators of competitiveness such as the index of revealed comparative advantage for this purpose.

First there has been a decline in the revealed competitiveness of agriculture (index values were steady between 1965 and 1975 then fell rapidly). Second, between 1979 and the end of the 1980s, there has been a rise and then a fall in the importance of mineral and energy exports, reflecting the cycle of international energy prices and their impact on the development and role of this sector in China. Third, there has been a rapid rise in the apparent competitiveness of labour-intensive products especially after 1985. Before then and even as far back as the second half of the 1960s, labour-intensive products (according to Zhang's product classification) accounted for some 40 per cent of exports. They rose to 55 per cent in a matter of a few years in the second half of the 1980s. The revealed comparative advantage index for exports of labour-intensive products also rose during this time.

Overall it appears that the substantial reforms to the international trading system in China led to a closer matching of comparative advantage and trade patterns. Warr and Zhang report that the correlation between the pattern of trade and estimated comparative advantage is weak in the early 1980s but that the correlation increases over the 1980s. While a contributing factor to the change was the reforms to the foreign trade system which were reviewed above, Findlay and Watson (1991), in their review of the recent experience of rural industry, also stress *a)* the high degree of export orientation of rural industry and *b)* the bias in their exports towards labour-intensive products. The rural industry sector boom will therefore create further pressures for adjustment in the agricultural sector, an effect which we examine in more detail later using the model results.

2.6.2 Agricultural Self Sufficiency

There has been considerable interest in the effects of reform on China's self sufficiency in agricultural products. The outcome depends on the complex interaction of three forces: the effects of sector-specific policies, the economy-wide effects of the management of the international trade system, and the long-run processes of growth.

Box 2.8 The Tea War

Since 1949, China has consistently exported over 30 per cent of its tea crop. Nearly all China's black tea is exported while most of the green tea output goes to the domestic market. Even so, China accounts for large shares of world trade in green tea. Tea exports are a major earner of foreign currency ($US421 million in 1989).

By the mid-1980s, there were a number of factors encouraging the liberalisation of tea marketing in China. These included the difficulties in getting the tea to markets under the centralised system, the low efficiency of that system and the high marketing costs, and the problems it created for competitiveness in the export market. In 1985, the export marketing system had been decentralised and the state distribution system then had to buy tea on contract in competition with other marketing systems. As in the case of wool, liberalising led to a boom in prices and the state responded by retreating from the previous reforms, reinstating a series of administrative levers. However the 'war' over tea supplies, taking the same forms as occurred in the wool and cotton markets, continued even into 1989 in some provinces.

Forster identifies a number of factors contributing to the tea war. These are also familiar from previous case studies. They include the development of processing capacity as a result of rural industrialisation, and the incentives for local governments to intervene in inter-regional trade to protect local industry. Also as in the wool case, the marketing reforms did not go far enough and did not encourage greater price variation according to tea quality. Producers continued to face greater incentives to produce quantity, rather than quality. The reinstatement of administrative controls as a result of the initial price rises reinforced this problem.

The devolution of responsibility for exports also added to the struggle for supplies. While the powers to manage exports were shifted to provincial governments, they were also given export targets to meet. The rise in prices in the first round of the war caused them to worry they would not be able to meet those targets at a profit. This provided another reason for intervening in the trade, especially for export tea. The forms of intervention included many protectionist measures designed to keep 'foreign' buyers out of local markets. The structure of incentives in the export marketing system therefore also contributed to the 'balkanisation' of the national tea market.

Furthermore, the intervention in order to meet export targets tended to lead to lower prices for export sales. Producers therefore had the incentive to try to continue to supply the domestic market where prices were higher. This was possible because the domestic market was dominated by green teas, not black teas which made up the bulk of exports. Processors therefore tried to switch from making green teas and it became even more difficult to meet the export targets. In addition, there was a large increase in the domestic stocks of green tea.

The first set of issues concerns the impact of sector-specific policies. There is a number of complications in assessing the effects of policy on resource allocation in China. First, infra-marginal distortions should not be included in those calculations. Procurement policies typically apply on infra-marginal purchases (Sicular, 1988), so they should not be counted[3]. While the main issue from the point of view of resource allocation is not therefore the transfers resulting from the quota price system, for some other purposes these gaps are important. Consumer prices are kept low through low procurement prices but in addition, consumer prices are subsidised by government. The extent of the gap between consumer prices, even infra-marginal prices, and world prices is of interest in this context.

From the point of view of resource allocation, however, the main issue is the effects of gaps at the margin between domestic and international prices. In addition, because of the role of the free markets, producers and consumers will at the margin face the same set of prices. The effects of border measures will therefore apply to both groups equally.

The impact of economy-wide distortions, in particular the presence of the two-tier exchange rate applying in China, further complicates the calculation of the extent of price distortion. As discussed in Martin (1990), the two-tier exchange rate system results from overvaluation of the official exchange rate. This overvaluation discourages exports, and a shortage of foreign exchange results. The scarce foreign exchange is rationed through the operation of secondary markets, where secondary market exchange rates are above the official exchange rate. The "equilibrium" exchange rate — that is, the rate that would be observed in the absence of the foreign exchange distortion — would lie between the official and the secondary market rates.

By estimating this equilibrium rate, it is possible to separate out the contributions of the foreign exchange system and the contribution of sector-specific policies to the gaps between domestic and world prices in each sector.

Estimates are reported in Chapter 4 where, in nearly every case, whether exportable or importable, there are sector-specific policies which reduce domestic agricultural prices in China below their foreign equivalent. In the case of imports, the absolute extent of this bias would be reduced by foreign exchange reform and by the appreciation that would be induced by that reform, but nearly all the measures of distortions indicate that domestic prices remain below world prices. This means that foreign exchange reform and the subsequent appreciation of the secondary market rate would lower the domestic equivalent of world prices but not by so much that actual domestic prices would then exceed the world price in domestic currency.

In the case of exports, domestic prices are generally below world prices. Foreign exchange reform would depreciate the official rate and raise the domestic equivalent of exportable goods prices. Thus the extent of the downward bias in domestic prices can only be increased by foreign exchange reform.

Further reforms in China which removed the sector-specific policies could actually increase domestic prices of both importables and exportables. This is suggested by the price distortion data discussed above. The net effect of those distortions is that exports are being taxed and that imports of agricultural goods are being subsidised. Reform would therefore remove the export tax and the import subsidy. The import-competing sector would expand and imports could fall. The export sector would grow and exports could increase. In that case the effects of a comprehensive trade policy reform on the agricultural sector in China at that time would be a substantial decline in net imports. The net agricultural trade position would improve. The significance of this result is therefore that in the short run, the effects of reform would have been to improve the degree of self sufficiency in the agricultural sector, not diminish it.

These are the immediate impacts of reform which lead to a rise in agricultural self sufficiency. The long-run forces work in the opposite direction. The decline of importance of the agricultural sector in an economy is common feature of development. The long-run factors contributing to agriculture's decline include: the effects of changes in income and population on the composition of demand and the effects of those shifts on prices, different rates of technological change between sectors, and changes in the national supplies of labour and capital and the impact of those changes on the structure of industry (Anderson, 1987, Martin and Warr, 1992). These sorts of forces would in the longer run be expected to reduce agricultural self sufficiency. We examine the empiricial significance of these long-run impacts of growth compared to the short-run effects of reform in later sections.

2.6.3 Political Economy of Reform

We noted the bias in pricing systems against the agricultural sector. What are the origins of this bias? The political influence of the urban residents over agricultural policy making is an important factor influencing the long-term trends in relative prices. Anderson (1990) notes the similarity of this pattern of discrimination against agriculture in other less developed economies, and the existence of the opposite pattern in industrialised economies. Anderson explains these outcomes in terms of the distributive effects of these policies. In particular, when agricultural products take up a large share of urban consumers' budgets then consumers have the incentive to take political action to resist price reforms. In China, before the reforms, this political bias was reinforced by Chinese ideas about the appropriate patterns of development. However there are forces which are unravelling the policy bias against agriculture.

As development proceeds so that

i) as the composition of household budgets changes, urban consumer sensitivity to agricultural product price rises is reduced: see Box 2.9 for detail of recent changes in patterns of consumer spending,

ii) as the size of the agricultural labour force shrinks, the costs of political action by the rural sector fall,

iii) structural change in the rural sector starts to impose more substantial adjustment costs on farmers, and generate some sympathy from urban households,

iv) the rate of import penetration starts to rise, heightening concerns about supply security,

then the policy tends to shift towards assistance for agriculture. The impact of some of these factors are some way off in China, but others either are already pressing on policy making, or will shortly be doing so. These include

- the rate of growth of import penetration, and,
- the shifts in household budgets.

The end result of the changes in the political forces is not clear. It may lead to high levels of protection for agriculture that are observed in other Northeast Asian economies. Over the time frame relevant here however the expectation is that the level

Box 2.9 The Composition of Household Budgets

Between 1981 and 1988 the share of food in per capita urban household spending fell from 57 per cent to 51 per cent. The Table shows the shifts in the composition of the food budget. The significant changes were the large fall in the share of grain in the food budget, from 23 per cent to 13 per cent. Significant increases also occurred in the shares of red meat (other than pork), poultry, eggs, fish and fruit. These data refer to urban households. In rural households the staple food share fell from 54 per cent in 1981 to 37 per cent in 1988.

Composition of Urban Household per capita Food Budgets (per cent)

	1981	1985	1988
Grain	23	17	13
Edible oil	4	4	4
Fresh vegetables	11	12	13
Pork	15	15	16
Beef & mutton	1	3	3
Poultry	2	4	5
Eggs	5	7	6
Fish	4	6	6
Tobacco, alcohol & tea	9	10	10
Fresh milk	1	1	1
Fruit	4	9	9
Other	21	12	14
Total	100	100	100

Budget composition changes over time reflect both income and price effects; however, the literature which has been able to separate these effects generally shows:

- a positive but small income elasticity of demand for foodgrain,
- positive and highly elastic demands for meat,
- high and positive income elasticities of demand for fruit and vegetables,
- even higher income elasticities of demand for milk and dairy products.

The implication is that as growth continues in China, the same trends in the composition of household budgets in the 1980s will continue into the 1990s. There may also be a greater demand within each group for higher-quality products. These trends have implications for the marketing arrangements for particular products which are examined in this chapter.

The change in the composition of household budgets is significant (e.g. the fall in the share of direct grain consumption). The World Bank (1990a) suggests that, on the basis of comparisons with consumption patterns in Taiwan over time, direct consumption of grain in China has peaked and is now expected to decline.

Source: State Statistical Bureau Household Survey Data.

of prices paid to producers will rise. Rising producer and consumer-relative prices at the margin for agricultural products would reduce the dependence of the Chinese economy on imports of those products.

2.6.4 Financial Impacts

The pattern of policy intervention and its impact on infra-marginal prices in the agricultural sector, while not directly significant for resource allocation, has severe financial implications for the government budget in China. Through this mechanism there could also be some indirect effects on resource allocation.

The extent of consumer subsidies rose from about 7 billion yuan in 1978 to a first peak of about 36 billion yuan in 1984 (about a quarter of total government revenue) then after a fall rose again to another high of more than 40 billion yuan in 1989[4]. This level of expenditure was difficult to sustain and in May 1991, as part of its campaign to cut back government spending, the Chinese government announced a wide range of subsidy cuts and, therefore, consumer price increases. Estimates of the price rises and the regional coverage of the price rises vary, but they appear to be concentrated in the grains group of products. It has been reported consistently that wheat, rice and corn prices rose, as did the price of cooking oil. The lowest reported price rise was of the order of 50 per cent. It is also reported, however, that there are still significant subsidies remaining. Indeed, subsidies attached to particular commodities have been replaced to some extent by a wages subsidy for urban residents, but not by enough to offset the price rises. This leads us to the issue of the control of government spending in China and macroeconomic management.

2.7 Macroeconomic Management of the Chinese Economy

In general over the 1980s, the macroeconomic performance of the Chinese economy was impressive. GDP growth averaged 9 per cent a year, and inflation rates were low. However, the process of decentralisation of the Chinese economy which was so important for fostering growth also led to some problems of macroeconomic imbalances. In particular, in the last two years of the 1980s there was a rapid increase in the inflation rate and a blow-out in the external deficit.

The institutions for macroeconomic control and the policy instruments themselves are under development in China. The ability of the central government to achieve macroeconomic control has been hampered by the reform process. For example, the process of decentralisation reduced the central government's share of revenue, so its capacity to influence the level of domestic spending through its fiscal policy was reduced. The autonomy given to regional governments, over investment in particular, and the slow pace of development of hard budget constraints in state enterprises and in the banking system, led to an explosion in the demand for funds. Provincial governments exerted some influence over the banking system in these circumstances, and enterprises were more dependent on bank lending for investment, given the decline in the share of funds for investment coming from government budgets.

The extent of decentralisation has increased over the 1980s but this has led to a faster growth in demand in each upswing of the macroeconomic cycle. The final result was a period of very rapid growth of the money supply in 1987 and 1988 associated with the problems noted above, that is, high rates of inflation and a rising current account deficit.

Once the seriousness of the problem became apparent, the central government was able to win the support of lower levels of government for its austerity programme. This programme involved a reinstatement of administrative measures, for example administrative allocation of credit, tightening of the indirect instruments of credit control such as reserve requirements, direct controls on prices and marketing, a cut-back on investment projects (which also led to many rural residents losing jobs in the construction sector and leaving the cities), controls over wage increases, and attempts to reduce the inflationary expectations of the urban population by announcing a slow-down in the pace of price reform.

These initiatives were very effective on this occasion but they contained a contradiction. While they dealt with the immediate crisis they represented a retreat from a more market-orientated economy. That retreat increases rather than decreases the likelihood of such crises occurring again in the future.

These methods of macroeconomic control in such a partially reformed economy have important implications for the speed of microeconomic reform. They also have implications for the allocation of resources between sectors of the economy. For example, the administration of credit controls also involved the targeting of particular sectors for priority. The government tried to limit credit available to rural industry through the formal banking system. The government also reimposed fixed price controls in markets for politically sensitive products like some foods, although there was considerable variation between regions in the management of price controls.

Variation in the money supply in a partially reformed economy can also have significant effects on resource allocation. In the absence of nominal price rigidities, changes in the money supply would change all nominal prices by the same amount, so that relative prices would be unaffected. In the Chinese economy, however, the fixed official exchange rate is an extremely important and pervasive nominal rigidity. The official exchange rate affects the price received for export goods. Changes in the general price level must therefore affect relative prices of broad categories of goods in China. A consequence of an increase in the money supply is a rise in the secondary market exchange rate (depreciation) which raises the price at the margin of imports and of their substitutes. The domestic prices of exportables also rise but by less (because the export price depends on the official exchange rate with a weight of only 75 per cent). As a result, the gap widens between prices obtained for exports and for import substitutes, and this further distorts the pattern of production.

2.8 Conclusions

In this chapter we have focused on the process of agricultural marketing reform in a number of major commodities, using that discussion to analyse the origins of the rapid growth in agricultural output following the first stage of the reforms and the scope for further reforms to raise productivity. Common aspects of the process of reform were cycles of de-regulation and the reinstatement of controls, and the 'balkanisation' of many agricultural markets. This problem of barriers to inter-regional trade tends to exaggerate the instability in urban markets, reinforcing the cycles of reform and re-regulation. The origins of the barriers to inter-regional trade lie in the partial nature of the reforms. One example is the different rates of de-regulation in various markets which leads to a continued bias against raw materials production compared to processing, and the incentives this creates for local governments to intervene in order to protect local interests. Another example is the devolution of power in an international trade system which retains the administrative mechanism of quantity targets.

Factors which may contribute to further productivity growth identified in this chapter include:

- the removal of internal barriers to trade, associated with various commodity wars, which will promote the pursuit of regional comparative advantage;
- the development of marketing institutions which will also promote the development of national markets for agricultural products;
- access to new varieties of grains and other technical inputs which will raise yields;
- more secure land tenure and land transfer arrangements which will facilitate the structural adjustments in agriculture following the rural industrial boom.

Economy-wide policies also have important implications for agriculture. The reforms to the international trading system have prompted the rapid increase in the international orientation of the Chinese economy, and even though substantial trade barriers remain, there is now a closer matching of China's comparative advantage and trade patterns. The expectation in a relatively resource-poor economy such as China is that in the long run the share of agricultural products in exports will fall and that agricultural self-sufficiency will also fall.

The short-run impacts of reform could, however, be different. The combination of distorted prices and the effects of the exchange rate system have been to tax both export and import-competing parts of the agricultural sector. The dynamic effects of growth are likely to lead to further price reforms (and removal of sector-specific price distortions), as the balance of forces in the political economy of policy-setting changes.

Agriculture is also affected by the macroeconomic management of the Chinese economy. In general over the 1980s, the macroeconomic performance of China was impressive. However the process of decentralisation that was an integral part of the reforms led to some problems of macroeconomic imbalances. The institutions for macroeconomic control are still under development in China. The instruments that are used (credit controls, price controls) can have direct impacts on the rural sector and on agriculture. In addition the distortions associated with these sorts of intervention and with the exchange rate system also mean that macroeconomic changes can have effects on the pattern of rural production which reduce welfare and growth.

Notes and References

1. The real farm land area is estimated to be some 2.0 billion mu, but the statistical number is about 1.6 billion mu, a difference of about 25 to 30 per cent. (If actual output is observed, but actual sown area is not, then the estimated yield will be too high.)
2. In 1984, the official yuan per US dollar rate was about 3. The official rate in October 1992 was over 5 yuan per dollar.
3. Marginal prices determine output in the short run. However in the long run, infra-marginal prices will influence investment decisions and the level of quasi-fixed factor inputs which will only be invested if their owners expect a residual return equal to what could be earned in other uses. In this longer-term context, any additional infra-marginal taxation imposed on agriculture can be expected to increase the outflow of resources from the agricultural sector, and to discourage investment.
4. These data are taken from Anderson (1990a), Table 5.1, and Webb (1991).

Table 2.1. **Sources of Growth in China's Agricultural Sector, 1978-1987**

(annual average rates: per cent shares in brackets)

	1978-84	1985-87
Output	6.1 (100)	0.7 (100)
Input	2.7 (41)	0.4 (55)
Productivity	2.9 (44)	0.7 (105)
Residual	1.1 (16)	-0.4 (-60)

Source: Lin (1989).

Chapter 3

The China Agriculture in General Equilibrium Model

3.1 Introduction

The introduction of the Household Responsibility System in agriculture was one of the early, and fundamental, elements of China's economic reforms. The reforms transformed Chinese agriculture from a sector subject to detailed microeconomic control to a much more productive one in which individual producing households are responsible for a wide range of their production and marketing decisions. In the post-reform environment, policy affects outcomes in the sector largely indirectly, by influencing the incentives faced by farmers and consumers. These incentives are also strongly influenced by a range of policy and non-policy factors whose effects are frequently indirect and difficult to evaluate without an appropriate model.

Agricultural price policies exert a direct and important influence on the Chinese agricultural sector. Other policies with a major impact on the sector include macroeconomic policy instruments such as the exchange rate setting, monetary policy, and spending and investment levels. Further, the performance and structure of the sector is heavily influenced by institutional changes and the development and adoption of technology in the farm and non-farm sectors of the economy. Perhaps one of the most important institutional changes affecting the agricultural sector in China was the reforms to property rights and the development of decentralized control mechanisms which allowed the emergence of a thriving township, village and private industry sector (Byrd and Lin, 1990). This development greatly improved the productivity of resources in rural industry and drew rural resources away from agriculture towards light industry and services, with important but poorly understood implications for the performance of the agricultural sector.

The China Agriculture in General Equilibrium (CAGEM) model was developed to allow the analysis of these major policy impacts in a fully general equilibrium context. The model builds on recent theoretical advances in understanding the performance and behaviour of the post-reform Chinese economy (Sicular, 1988; Byrd, 1987) and on earlier general equilibrium models of the Chinese economy developed by one of the authors (Martin, 1991a).

The model is built around an input-output table for the Chinese economy built up from a general input-output table and a specialized table for the Chinese agricultural sector. To our knowledge, it provides the first complete empirical framework for analyzing the impacts of both macroeconomic and sectoral (including agricultural and industrial) policies on the Chinese agricultural sector. The model enforces consistency on the interaction of the various policy instruments, a consistency which is difficult to achieve using simpler models given the complex web of interacting policy interventions in the Chinese economy.

Since the model is based heavily on the theoretical formulations of the two-tier pricing system for pricing in the domestic market advanced by Sicular (1988), Byrd (1987) and Wu and Zhao (1989), and on the rather different two-tier pricing system prevailing in the market for foreign exchange (Martin, 1990), these features of the Chinese economy are discussed in the next section. The basic structure of the model is then considered in section 3.3. The structural representation of the agricultural sector is considered in more detail in section 3.4. The equations and parameters of the model are discussed in section 3.5.

3.2 Broad Economic Structure

One of the main features of the economic reforms in China since 1978 has been the replacement of a pure planning system by a two-tier pricing system. Under this two-tier system, producing enterprises receive payment for some of their output at prices fixed by the state but, once having met this constraint, are able to sell the remainder of their output on secondary markets at relatively flexible prices. Similarly, consumers are frequently able to purchase some part of their demands (eg. food rations) at state-fixed prices but, in addition, have access to secondary markets for additional purchases at a higher, market-determined price.

From microeconomic theory, we know that a profit maximizing producer's decision on total output levels will not be affected by the requirement to deliver a fixed quantity of output, or a fixed value of profits, to the state. Only the marginal return on output enters the first order conditions for profit maximization and a fixed delivery quota or, equivalently, a lump-sum tax, will not affect the marginal conditions. Similarly, the input decisions of cost-minimizing enterprises will not be affected by the state providing a fixed allocation of inputs at state-determined prices.

The consumer case is similar to the producer case considered above. Consumer decisions are guided by the marginal cost of obtaining additional units of a good, or the marginal return from selling additional units, rather than by the average price, or some infra-marginal price such as the price applying on a limited ration quantity. When analyzing the effect on the consumer, however, the redistribution of income brought about by the rationing system must be considered. The receivers of allocations at below-market prices receive a transfer (the provision of which is the main purpose of the system) and this transfer raises their effective incomes and, presumably, their spending levels. Thus the two-tier pricing system can be expected to have a direct impact on the consumption levels and consumption patterns of particular groups. However, since the system involves transfers from one group to another, the increase in total spending by the benefited group will be offset by a decrease in spending by the group which finances the transfers. There will only be an effect on the overall pattern of consumption if the spending patterns of the benefited groups are systematically different from the spending patterns of the group which pays for the transfers.

Under a pure planning system, where producers are rigidly constrained by the quantity of inputs they are allocated, and where consumers can consume only their ration quantities of consumption goods, prices play no role in the allocation of goods, and factors and economic outcomes are entirely determined by the planning process. Under partial liberalization, plan allocations will continue to play a role in determining economic outcomes if producers or consumers are constrained to produce or consume these quantities.

As Sicular (1988) has pointed out, the presence of secondary markets greatly extends the range of situations in which the two-tier pricing model is applicable. A consumer who receives a food ration larger than his/her demand at the secondary market price can choose to sell some of this ration on the secondary market. Where direct sale of ration cards is not allowed, this may require a little circumspection, or a barter transaction in the market, but such welfare-enhancing transactions are reported to occur very widely. The effective unit price, at the margin, for a consumer with excess ration cards is the same as the consumer with too few, or no, ration cards. For the consumer with excess ration cards, it is the official price for rationed goods plus the opportunity cost of not selling the ration cards. Given active arbitrage in the market for ration coupons, this total cost will be essentially the same as the secondary market price. For the consumer with too few ration cards, it will be the secondary market price or, equivalently, the price of additional ration cards plus the official price. Exactly the same situation arises for enterprises purchasing inputs.

The theoretical model of domestic pricing and resource allocation sketched above is undoubtedly too simple to account for the full complexity of the post-reform Chinese economy. There must be some doubt about how consistently enterprises attempt to maximize profits, rather than some other, less clear-cut goal. Moreover the Central, Provincial and local authorities in China frequently intervene in a variety of ways which adversely affect the ability of the secondary markets to perform their intended functions. Efficient arbitrage activities are frequently criticized as unproductive speculation. Efficiency-improving resource transfers between enterprises or regions are frequently made illegal and forced into indirect (barter) transfers or into black markets. Output quotas are sometimes seen to depend upon the level of output, introducing a link between the state delivery quota and the level of output. Only the assumption that consumers consistently attempt to maximize utility seems unassailable.

Despite these important objections, the two-tier pricing model appears likely to be an extremely useful means of generating insights into the behaviour of the Chinese economy. The decentralization of decision making to producing enterprises has been a major, continuing thrust of the economic reforms since 1978. Secondary markets, organized and informal, legal and otherwise, are widespread in China and play a vital role in re-allocating producer inputs and consumer goods, and providing incentives both to producers and consumers. Acceptance of this model does not imply an absence of intervention in the economy. A wide range of policy interventions influencing the economy can be analyzed within this very general framework.

Broad acceptance of the two-tier pricing model as a useful framework permits the use of relatively straightforward techniques for modelling the behaviour of the economy. Only the secondary market prices matter for resource allocation, and hence the complex and confusing system of multi-tier official prices can largely be bypassed.

Unfortunately, this simplification needs to be modified in order to analyze the foreign exchange and foreign trade system. The two-tier pricing system for foreign exchange is quite different from the system prevailing in domestic markets (Martin, 1990). Furthermore, a wide variety of interventions, e.g. on the enterprises which can conduct foreign trade, import quotas, licensing and tariffs (World Bank, 1988), all introduce distortions between international prices and domestic secondary market prices.

The two-tier pricing system for foreign exchange in China is similar in principle to those found in many developing countries with highly controlled foreign trade regimes. The official exchange rate has typically been substantially overvalued, reducing the domestic currency returns obtained by exporters and hence their willingness to supply exports. At the same time, the overvalued currency reduces the apparent cost of imports and stimulates the *ex ante* demand for imports.

The implications of this controlled, and overvalued, foreign exchange system can be illustrated by a simple diagram such as that presented in Figure 3.1. In the figure, the equilibrium exchange rate, e^*, is determined by the intersection of the supply and demand curves for foreign exchange. The resulting supply of foreign exchange, q^*, is the equilibrium at which the supply and the demand for foreign exchange are equated. Overvaluing the yuan by reducing the official price of foreign exchange to e_o reduces the supply of foreign exchange to q_s by reducing the incentive to export. The consequent shortage of foreign exchange causes the secondary market exchange rate to depreciate to e_2.

The system is enforced through a system of exchange controls under which the recipients of foreign exchange are required to sell their foreign exchange to a state agency, the State Administration of Exchange Control. Foreign exchange is then made available for use within enterprises and local governments through a system of foreign exchange retention rights (Chan, 1991). The share of foreign exchange which an exporting enterprise can retain has varied widely depending upon the nature of the enterprise, its location and the commodity being exported. Recently, however, the system of retention rights has been streamlined to reduce the variability between enterprises and regions. Under the new system, exporters of general commodities retain up to 70 per cent of their foreign exchange earnings, the local government receives 10 per cent and the central government receives only 20 per cent with an option to purchase an additional 30 per cent at the secondary market rate (Chan, 1991). Retained foreign exchange may usually be used by the enterprise itself, subject to import licensing and quota controls, to purchase imports, or may be sold on secondary markets for foreign exchange.

Increases in the foreign exchange retention rate over time have reduced the adverse implications of the foreign exchange system for exports and for economic performance generally. However, a more important mitigating factor has been the progressive reductions in the degree of exchange rate overvaluation in recent years. The percentage difference between the official and the secondary market exchange rates has narrowed from over 80 per cent in mid-1989 to in the order of 10 per cent in 1990 and 1991 (Martin, 1991b, p. 3).

Since the price of foreign exchange on the secondary markets is invariably higher than the official exchange rate, the ability to retain foreign exchange increases the domestic currency returns to exporting enterprises. This, in turn, can be expected to increase the supply of exports, and hence the aggregate supply of foreign exchange.

The foreign trade system remained relatively tightly controlled in China despite the generally rapid rate of economic reform, with Foreign Trade Corporations (FTCs) typically acting as intermediaries between producers and foreign buyers. However, the "air-lock" between domestic producers and foreign purchasers of exports has been substantially reduced with a dramatic increase in the number of Foreign Trade Corporations and with some larger firms allowed direct trading rights. On the import side, it is reported that most imports are now made on an agency system where the price charged to the purchaser is based upon the foreign exchange cost, the exchange rate and a handling charge for the Foreign Trade Corporation. On the export side, official procurement prices have typically been set domestically allowing them to get out of line with world market returns. However, the ability for Foreign Trade Corporations to maintain distorted prices has come under increased pressure as competition between FTCs has increased, particularly now that export subsidies have been abolished (Lardy, 1991).

3.3 Structure of the Model

As discussed above, the theoretical underpinning of the model is the theory of two-tier pricing espoused by Sicular (1988), Byrd (1987) and Wu and Zhao (1987). Under this form of two-tier pricing system, production and consumption levels are guided by secondary market prices, while plan quotas and rations have only a distributional effect. This theory implies that a model such as the present one, with a focus on allocative effects of policies, need only consider secondary market prices except where redistributions of income through the planning system have allocative effects through differences in spending propensities. Further, it implies that the behaviour of economic agents can be modelled as responding to marginal market incentives in the same way as agents in an explicitly market-oriented economy.

On this basis, the model is explicitly neoclassical in spirit, with consumers modelled as maximizing utility subject to available income, and producers minimizing the costs of producing particular patterns of output and maximizing returns for a particular level of output in multi-output firms. The model is designed to focus on the impacts of policy measures and other shocks on production output and prices. While it would be desirable to be able to track the implications of the major taxes and transfers implicit in the two-tier pricing system, together with the more conventional tax and transfer systems, this was seen as being a high cost objective, and not central to the major objectives of the study. As a consequence, the model was constructed with an emphasis on the real side of the economy, with no attempt to capture the revenue implications of policies, and with real spending levels either held constant or varied exogenously.

Because of this simplification, common in models of the ORANI type (Dixon, *et al.*, 1982), the primary data requirement for the construction of the model was an input-output model of the Chinese economy, rather than a more comprehensive Social Accounting Matrix.

The final input-output table utilized in the study is presented in Appendix Table A3.1. The basic input-output information was obtained from the 1985 World Bank study (World Bank, 1985, p. 51). Since the initial table, for 1981, was expressed in official prices, and secondary market prices were required for a model of this type, a series of price adjustments was undertaken. The details of this procedure are given in Thompson (1990). The resulting input-output table at market prices was used as the starting point for the preparation of the basic table utilized in this study. However, for the purposes of this study, a considerably more disaggregated characterization of the agricultural sector was required. The benchmark data-set on which the analysis is based was constructed by systematically combining data from a range of sources, using procedures discussed in Appendix 3.1.

Most of the required additional information on the technical structure of the agricultural sector was obtained from the 1982 input-output table for the agricultural sector prepared by Chen, Hao and Xue (1986). Their table in value units includes a total of 24 agricultural sectors, allowing considerable freedom in the choice of sectors to be included in the model. The information contained in the agricultural input-output table was supplemented with information from other sources, such as the World Bank study of the livestock sector (1987), to prepare the complete input-output table presented in Appendix Table A3.1. Since one of the activities or sectors, the crops sector, has multiple outputs, there are more commodities than activities in the model. A complete list of the 29 model sectors and 38 model commodities is given in Table 3.1.

The consumer income elasticities for each commodity were based primarily on the estimates used in the construction of the World Bank's dynamic input-output model of China (World Bank, 1985a, p. 28) and used in an earlier, less finely disaggregated, model of the Chinese economy (Martin, 1991a). To allow for the greater degree of disaggregation required in the present study, additional income elasticities for agricultural commodities were drawn from Anderson and Tyers (1987, p. 147) and from World Bank (1987, pp. 139-140). The resulting "consensus" estimates of income elasticities were then re-scaled slightly to ensure that the Engel aggregation condition held at base-period consumer expenditure shares. The final elasticity estimates are presented in Table 3.1.

The functional forms chosen for the model are the Linear Expenditure System for consumer demand; the Leontief form for intermediate input demand; the Constant Elasticity of Substitution (CES) for primary factor input demands and import demands; and the Constant Elasticity of Transformation (CET) for output transformation in multi-output production processes.

The model is linear in percentage changes and solved by Johansen's linearization using the GEMPACK programme (Codsi and Pearson, 1988). The use of linear functional forms greatly assists in the solution of a relatively large model and allows great flexibility in adapting the model to the problem considered. It also leads to results which are expressed in extremely convenient reduced-form elasticities of response. The main disadvantage of this approach is the possibility that, for very large shocks, some degree of linearization error will be introduced. Experience with this type of model suggests that these errors are likely to be small, particularly relative to errors resulting from inaccurate selection of parameter values (Dixon *et al.*, 1982). If necessary, and at the cost of considerable additional parameter updating, these errors can be eliminated by solving the model in a series of small steps.

The basic version of the model used in this study is short-run in character, with exogenous capital stocks in each industry. While models of this type are typically used to analyse the comparative static effects of policy changes, their formulation in percentage change form allows them to be used to analyse steady-state growth paths under varying assumptions about exogenous variables (to the model) such as investment and rates of technical change.

3.4 Equations and Parameters of the Model

The set of equations making up the model is presented in Table 3.2, together with the definitions of the variables and coefficients. Throughout the table, lower case letters represent variables, Greek characters are parameters, and upper case characters refer to value shares. Each of the equation sets is discussed in turn below.

The first six sets of equations specify the final demands for goods and the demands for intermediate goods by each sector. The first set of equations specifies the demands for each good by households as a function of household disposable income and the (marginal) prices of each good. In the absence of any elasticity estimates based on the appropriate marginal prices, the set of elasticities was calculated using expenditure elasticities for each good (World Bank, 1985b), budget share data at market prices, and an estimate of the Frisch Parameter (-6.9) obtained by interpolating from the international estimates provided by Lluch, Powell and Williams (1977). By virtue of the method used in their construction (Dervis, de Melo and Robinson, 1981, pp. 482-5), the resulting estimates satisfy the theoretical constraints on demand systems: homogeneity of degree zero in prices and income, symmetry and adding up.

Equation sets (2), (3) and (4) specify proportional changes in fixed investment, investment in stocks and government consumption demands for each commodity as determined by the proportional changes in gross real absorption in the economy or by exogenous shift variables. In the absence of exogenous shifts, the simple behavioural hypothesis of demand changing in line with total real absorption was chosen as a neutral benchmark given the considerable uncertainty about how these categories respond to relative prices. Exogenous shift variables have been incorporated in these equations to allow the effects of changes in the pattern of spending on these categories to be analyzed.

Equation set (5) summarizes China's trade environment. China's exports of each commodity i are represented using a CES function (linearized in percentage changes) consistent with the Armington (1969) model. The demand for exports of good i is determined by the prices of China's exports relative to exports from the rest of the world, and the total demand for exports of that commodity. In turn, world import demand was specified as a linear (in proportional changes) function of the weighted average price for good i, where the weights are the shares of China and the rest of the world in total exports of good i. The supply of imports is specified as a function of the world price of imports, allowing for the possibility of China being 'large' in particular markets.

Equation set (6) specifies the demands for intermediate inputs of commodities in the production process. For simplicity, and for consistency with most models of this type, intermediate inputs are, in the absence of technical changes, assumed to be used in fixed proportion to outputs, that is according to a Leontief technology. A wide range of specialized types of exogenous input-augmenting technical change are incorporated in this equation. The first technical change variable (ah) refers to Hicks-Neutral input and factor-augmenting technical change applying to all inputs in all sectors. The second (ah_j) refers to sector-specifc improvement in the efficiency of all inputs. The third (ai_i) variable refers to an input-specific reduction in the permit requirements of a specific input in all sectors. The ai_{gk} variables allow for technical change which is differentiated both by input and by sector. Input saving technical change is represented by a decline in the relevant technical change variable.

Equation set (7) aggregates intermediate usage, household stocks, consumption and government demand into a total absorption variable for each good. Value share weights are used to convert this linear identity into percentage change form. Since export and domestic products are differentiated, export demand is not a component of total absorption of i.

Equation set (8) specifies imperfect substitution between domestic and imported products consistent with the Armington (1969) model. Equation set (9) introduces a corresponding treatment of domestic production — specifying imperfect transformation between domestically produced products supplied to domestic and export markets. This equation is a linearization in percentage changes of the constant elasticity of transformation (CET) function discussed in the context of CGE models by Robinson (1989).

Equation set 10(a) specifies the transformation possibilities from generalized output to individual commodities in each sector, according to a CET technology. While this transformation is specified for each sector in order to maintain consistency of equation structure across sectors, it is effective only in the crops sector. This is the only sector with multiple commodity outputs in the "make" matrix of commodity output per sector. Increases in the price of one commodity relative to the weighted average price of commodities will result in an increase in the output of that commodity relative to total sectoral output. A term (ac_i) for commodity-specific technical advance was also included in this equation. Equation set 10 (b) aggregates the production of commodities across sectors, using the value shares of each sector in the total output of each commodity (OA) as weights.

The specification of the technical change variables in Equation set (10) is based on a commodity augmenting technical change model. Producers are assumed to optimize over effective units of output, rather than physical units, where the relationship between effective units and physical units is:

$$C_{ij} = AC_i \, C_{ij}^*$$

where C_{ij} is the level of output of commodity i from sector j; C_{ij}* is the effective output level and AC_i is the level of commodity augmenting technical change defined so that an increase in AC_i represents a technical advance. The corresponding relationship between nominal and effective prices is:

$$P_i = P_i^*/AC_i$$

where P_i is the price of commodity i and P_i* is the effective price of commodity i. This relationship implies, logically, that output augmenting technical change will raise the effective price of the commodity at any given market price level. This impact of technical change on the effective price is captured in the model through the p_i and ac_i terms in Equation (10).

Equation set (11) specifies the demand for primary factor inputs by industry i as a function of the output level in industry i and the relative prices of each of the primary factor inputs (land, labour and capital). It is assumed that these inputs can be aggregated into a composite primary factor bundle using a CES function, and the demand equations are obtained by imposing the first order conditions for cost minimization and linearizing in percentage changes.

A set of factor-augmenting technical change variables corresponding to the input-augmenting technical change variables introduced in Equation set (6) appears in those primary factor input equations. In this case, however, these variables influence factor use in two ways: firstly through the direct reduction in factor demand resulting from an increase in the effective quantity of each input and, secondly, through the induced changes in factor demand resulting from the lower effective price of factors which have become more productive.

The factor demand equations are derived by specifying the CES production function in terms of "effective" factor inputs: $Q_{vj}^* = Q_{vj}/A_{vj}$, where Q_{vj}* is the effective input of factor v to sector j, Q_{vj} is the physical input of factor v, and A_{vj} is the technical change coefficient for factor v in industry j. A decline in A_{vj} increases the effective quantity of factor input v to industry j obtained from any given level of the physical factor input. An increase in the effective quantity of factor v per physical unit causes a *ceteris paribus* reduction in the effective price of this input. This relationship is expressed as:

$$P_{vj}^* = A_{vj} \,.\, P_{vj}$$

When effective prices are substituted for actual prices, and the input-substitution relationship is converted to percentage changes represented by lower case variables, Equation (11) is obtained.

The market clearing conditions for commodities are specified in Equation block (12). In 12(a), domestic demand for good i from domestic sources (q_{i2}) is equated with domestic production of good i for the home market (x_{i2}). Similarly, export demand for good i from China must equal Chinese production of good i for export (x_{i1}).

Equation set (13) deals with market clearing for primary factors. Equation 13(a) embodies the assumption, standard in models of this type, that labour is able to move between different industries in response to changes in the demand for labour. While this is undoubtedly a strong assumption given the constraints on the physical mobility of labour in China, the explosive growth of the lightly regulated rural industries in China has greatly increased the opportunities for labour to move between agriculture and industry, and between industrial sectors. The stock of capital in each industry, and the stock of land in each agricultural industry, are specified exogenously in 13(b) and 13(c).

Equation set (14) imposes the condition of zero pure profits on activities conducted at marginal (free market) prices. In production, this condition involves the inherent assumption of constant returns to scale — reasonable given the very large number of enterprises involved in most industrial (and certainly agricultural) activities in China. While the two-tier pricing system generates large profits and losses, these are assumed to be infra-marginal and hence irrelevant for short-run resource allocation. The technical change terms in these equations reflect the favourable effects of output-augmenting or input-saving technological advance on levels of returns and costs.

The zero-profit or arbitrage conditions in exporting and importing are of vital importance and therefore are examined in some detail. The condition for the import market is simply a linear in percentage change version of:

$$P_{i2} = P_{i}n(1 + T_{i}).\ \Phi_{2}$$

where P_{i2} is the landed, domestic currency price of imported good i, $P_{i}n$ is the 'world' price for imports of good i, T_i is the rate of tariff applying to imports of i (plus the tariff equivalent of any import quota) and Φ_2 is the secondary market exchange rate. At the margin, it is assumed that the opportunity cost of all imports involves the secondary market rate. If an enterprise has less foreign exchange demands, it must purchase additional foreign exchange in the secondary market. If it initially has more foreign exchange than it requires, its opportunity cost of using foreign exchange is also the secondary market rate.

In exporting, the returns available depend upon the foreign currency price received, the rate of any export tax, and a weighted average of the official and secondary market exchange rates. The higher the rate of retention allowed to enterprises, the larger the weight on the secondary market, and hence the higher the domestic currency price of exports. Equation 13(c) was derived by expanding the nonlinear export value equation about base period values for the retention rate and the official and secondary market exchange rates. It allows the effects of changes in both the official exchange rate and in the retention rate applied in each industry to be examined. The weight FES reflects the base retention rate of 0.25 which applied through most of the 1980s and allows the effects of recent changes from this level to be investigated.

Equation set (15) includes identities to form aggregate Gross Domestic Product and absorption in current and constant prices. Equation 15(c) is used to make aggregate real absorption an exogenous variable in the model. Equation 15(d) requires that total household consumption, and the spending associated with investment and government purchases, add to total absorption.

Equation set (16) defines the balance of trade, and Equation set (17) includes identities for trade volumes and values.

Equation set (18)(a) is a demand for money equation, with a unitary income elasticity of demand imposed. This equation essentially imposes the quantity theory of money and implies that a 1 per cent increase in the money supply will raise the Gross Domestic Product price deflator by 1 per cent. Chow (1987) finds evidence that the quantity theory applies reasonably well to China and in fact concluded that it appeared to offer a better representation of price behaviour for China than for the USA.

While Chow's results did not support the strict quantity theory result that an increase in the money supply would have an equiproportional effect on the price level, this result may have reflected the stickiness of official prices over much of his sample period. Feltenstein and Ziba (1987, p. 153) conclude that the official price indices of the type used by Chow substantially understated the true rate of inflation. If their estimate of the true rate of inflation in China (2.5 times the official rate) is combined with the estimate by Chow that a 1 per cent increase in the money supply would raise official prices by one-third of 1 per cent, the unit elasticity used in this study appears reasonable. Institutions for management of monetary policy are evolving to provide greater scope for exogenous policy control of the money supply.

The final five equations of the model 18(b)-18(e) define the price of each of the composite goods (import plus domestic sources goods) consumed domestically, and the price of composite goods (export plus domestic destination goods) produced domestically and composite prices for total absorption and total Gross Domestic Product.

The complete model contains 3 113 equations, and 3 113 endogenous variables. The model is linear in percentage changes and was solved using the GEMPACK programme (Codsi and Pearson, 1988).

In addition to the input-out data discussed above, the model requires that a number of elasticity parameters be specified. The elasticities involved were:

- consumer demand elasticities;
- elasticities of substitution between domestic and imported good i (Base value 2.0);
- elasticities of transformation between crop commodities in the crops sector (Base value 2.0);
- elasticities of transformation between domestic and export good i (Base value 5.0);
- elasticities of substitution between Chinese exports of i and the exports of other countries (Base value 10.0);
- the elasticity of demand for total world exports of i (Base value -2.0);
- the elasticity of supply of import i to China (Base value 100); and
- the elasticity of substitution between primary factors in industry i (Base value 0.5).

As previously discussed, the consumer demand elasticities were derived using expenditure elasticities, budget shares and the Frisch parameter. It seemed unlikely that reasonable estimates of the elasticities of substitution and transformation for each commodity could be estimated satisfactorily using the available data for China. Time series of the relevant market price data are extremely scarce and, in any event, the time period over which enterprise managers have been free to allocate their resources in response to relative price changes is short. Accordingly, the approach taken was to impose selected base values chosen on the basis of the evidence from other countries, leaving open the option of examining the sensitivity of the results obtained to these assumptions.

The base value of 2.0 used for the elasticity of substitution between domestic and imported commodities is within the range of values used for this parameter in CGE studies. While the values used in the Grais, de Melo and Urata (1986) study range only from 0.4 to 1.2, the corresponding parameters are larger in many other CGE studies. If one accepts the weight of empirical evidence marshalled by Goldstein and Khan (1985, p. 1076) that the aggregate elasticity of import demand is in the range -0.5 to -1.0, and if one accepts that own price elasticities for individual commodities are likely to be higher than the aggregate elasticity, then an elasticity of substitution of 2.0 at the individual commodity level would seem entirely reasonable.

Unfortunately, the empirical evidence on the elasticity of transformation between domestic and export production is extremely limited. The estimate of 2.90 cited by Tarr (1989, p. 5-6) provides some indication of the order of magnitude, at least for manufactured products. While well below the value of infinity implicit in models constructed without explicit transformation in production, it is well above the values of 0.5 and 1.5 assumed by Grais, de Melo and Urata (1986). The evidence that the aggregate supply elasticity of exports may lie in the range from 1.0 to 4.0 (Goldstein and Khan, 1985, p. 1087) also seems to point to higher values for this parameter than those chosen by Grais, de Melo and Urata (1986, p. 74). The value of 5.0 for individual commodities used in this study was subjectively set somewhat above the empirically estimated aggregate values, given the well-known downward bias in these estimates resulting from the pervasive problem of measurement errors.

The elasticities of substitution between exports from China and other export products were set at 10.0 in the belief that Chinese exports of many products are close substitutes for other products in world markets. This assumption is higher than the few available direct estimates of the elasticity of export demand for China's exports, but the likelihood that such estimates are biased downwards is well known (see, for example, Leamer and Stern, 1970, p. 56-74). For commodity exports, at least, the value of 10.0 does not seem unreasonable, and is broadly consistent with values used in many other CGE modelling exercises (eg., Dixon *et al.*, 1982).

The base value elasticity of demand for total world exports was set at -2.0 in the light of the relatively low elasticity of substitution between domestic and imported goods assumed in the model. Since the focus of the model is on a relatively short time period, supply adjustment in other countries may be fairly low, placing the major burden of adjustment on world demand. Given China's small share of world exports, the elasticity of demand for her exports would generally be expected to depend more heavily on the elasticity of substitution than the overall market elasticity of demand.

The very high base value for the elasticity of supply of imports to China was chosen to make China essentially a price taker in the market for imports. Given China's small share in most markets this does not appear unreasonable as a working assumption.

The elasticity of substitution between primary factors was set to a base value of 0.5. This value was selected by Dixon *et al.*, (1982) after an extensive literature search. While it is substantially below some of the estimates presented in the developing country literature (e.g. Limskul, [1988]) it does not seem unreasonable as a short-run estimate, particularly when the effects of any constraints on adjustment resulting from the operation of the planning system are considered.

The model developed in this section is used in Chapter 4 to analyze the effects of major shocks affecting Chinese agricultural sector.

Table 3.1. **Sectors, Commodities and Consumer Income Elasticities in the China Agriculture in General Equilibrium Model**

Sectors	Commodities	Consumer Income Elasticities
Crops	Rice	0.11
Crops	Wheat	0.47
Crops	Other grains	-0.11
Crops	Tuber crops	0.11
Crops	Soybeans and oils	0.74
Crops	Cotton and hemp	0.0
Crops	Sugar and tobacco	0.66
Crops	Tea, fruits and vegetables	0.84
Crops	Other crops	0.42
Crops	Forestry	0.0
Cattle	Cattle	0.78
Pigs	Pigs	0.85
Poultry	Poultry	0.69
Sheep	Sheep	0.78
Fisheries	Fisheries	0.78
Metallurgy	Metallurgy	0.0
Electricity	Electricity	2.65
Coal	Coal	0.47
Oil mining	Oil mining	1.28
Oil refining	Oil refining	1.00
Chemicals	Chemicals	1.57
Chemical fibres	Chemical fibres	0.0
Machinery	Machinery	1.64
Building materials	Building materials	0.0
Wood	Wood	0.0
Food processing	Food processing	1.50
Textiles	Textiles	1.27
Apparel	Apparel	1.27
Paper	Paper	0.0
Misc. manufacturing	Misc. manufacturing	1.74
Construction	Construction	0.0
Freight transport	Freight transport	1.62
Passenger transport	Passenger transport	0.0
Commerce	Commerce	1.28
Misc. services	Misc. services	1.57
Education and health	Education and health	1.21
Public administration and health	Public administration and health	0.0
Housing	Housing	1.57

Table 3.2. **Model Equations and Variables**

1. *Household Consumption Demands*

$$q_i^{(3)} = \epsilon_i a^* + \sum_{k=1}^{g} \eta_{ik} p_k^q$$

g

2. *Fixed Investment Demand*

$$q_i^{(2)} = a_R + ff_i$$

g

3. *Investment in Stocks*

$$qs_i^{(2)} = a_R + fs_i$$

g

4. *Government Demand*

$$q_i^{(5)} = a_R + gd_i$$

g

5. *Traded Good Demand/Supply*

(a) Export Demand from China

$$q_i^{(4)} = qw_1^{(4)} - \sigma_i^w (p_{i1}^e - \sum_{s=1}^{2} ES_{is} p_{is}^e)$$

g

(b) World Demand

$$qw_i^{(4)} = \beta_i (\sum_{s=1}^{2} ES_{is} p_{is}^e)$$

g

(s = 1, China; 2, Rest of World)

(c) Import Supply to China

$$q_{is} = E_i p_i^m$$

g

6. *Intermediate Demand*

$$q_{ij}^{(1)} = x_j + ah + ah_j + ai_i + ai_{ij}$$

gh

7. *Domestic Absorption of Good i from all Sources*

$$q_i = \Sigma_j B_{ij}^{(1)} q_{ij}^{(1)} + B_i^{(2)} q_i^{(2)} + BS_i^{(2)} qs_i^{(2)} + B_i^{(3)} q_i^{(3)} + B_i^{(5)} q_i^{(5)}$$

g

8. *Domestic/Import Substitution*

$$q_{is} = q_i - \sigma_i^m (p_{is} - p_i^q) \qquad 2g$$

(s = 1, imported; 2, domestic)

9. *Domestic/Export Transformation*

$$cd_{id} = c_i + \sigma_i^T (p_{id} - p_i^x) \qquad 2g$$

(d = 1, export; 2, domestic)

10. *Commodity Output*

$$(a) \quad c_{ij} = x_j + \sigma_j^c (p_i^x - \sum_{n=1}^{g} GR_{nj} p_n^x)$$

$$+ac_i + \sigma_j^c (ac_c - \sum_{n=1}^{g} GR_{nj} ac_n) \qquad gh$$

$$(b) \quad c_i = \sum_{j=1}^{h} OA_{ij} c_{ij} \qquad g$$

11. *Primary Factor Inputs*

$$q_{vj}^p = x_j - \sigma_i^p (p_{vj}^p - \sum_{w=1}^{3} S_{wj}^p p_{wj}^p)$$

$$+ah+ah_j+af+af_v+af_{vj} \qquad 3h$$

$$-\sigma_i^p (af_v + af_{vj} - \sum_{w=1}^{3} S_{wj}^p (af_w + af_{wj}))$$

12. *Product Market Clearing*

(a) Domestic market clearing

$$q_{i2} = cd_{i2} \qquad g$$

(b) Export market clearing

$$q_i^{(4)} = cd_{i1} \qquad g$$

13. *Factor Market Clearing*

$$(a) \quad q_i^p = \Sigma_{j=1}^{g} L_j q_{1j} \qquad \text{- Labour} \qquad 1$$

$$(b) \quad q_{2j}^p = k_j \qquad \text{- Capital in i} \qquad h$$

(c) $q^{p}_{3j} = l_j$ - Land in i h

14. *Zero Pure Profits at the Margin*

(a) In Production

$$\Sigma_s GR_{sj} p^{x}_{s} + \Sigma_s GR_{sj} ac_s = \sum_{i=1}^{g} H^{(1)}_{ij} p^{q}_{i}$$
$$+ \sum_{i=1}^{g} H^{(1)}_{ij} (a^{i}_{i} + a^{i}_{ij}) + \sum_{v=1}^{3} H^{p}_{vj} p^{p}_{vj} + \sum_{v=1}^{3} HP^{p}_{vj} af_v$$
$$+ \sum_{v=1}^{3} HP^{p}_{vj} af_{vj} + ah + ah_j$$

h

(b) In Importing

$$p_{i2} = p^{m}_{i} + t_i + \varnothing_2$$

g

(c) In Exporting

$$p_{i1} = p^{e}_{i} + v_i + FES_1(RC*rr_i + \varnothing_1)$$
$$+ (1-FES_1)(rr_i + \varnothing_2)$$

g

15. *GDP, Absorption and Household Absorption*

(a)

$$gdp_r = \Sigma_i G^{(3)}_{i} q^{(3)}_{i} + \Sigma_i G^{(2)}_{i} q^{(2)}_{i}$$
$$+\Sigma_i GS^{(2)}_{i} qs^{(2)}_{i} + \Sigma_i G^{(5)}_{i} q^{(5)}_{i}$$
$$+\Sigma_i G^{(4)}_{i} . q^{(4)}_{i} - \Sigma_i G^{(6)}_{i} . q_{i1}$$

1

(b)

$$gdp = \Sigma_i G_i^{(3)} (p_i^q + q_i^{(3)}) + \Sigma_i G_i^{(2)} (p_i^q + q_i^{(2)}) + \Sigma_i GS_i^{(2)} (p_i^q + qs_i^{(2)}) + \Sigma G_i^{(5)} (p_i^q + q_i^{(5)}) + \Sigma G_i^{(4)} (p_i^q + q_i^{(4)}) - \Sigma G_i^{(6)} (p_i^q + q_{i1}) \quad 1$$

(c)

$$a_R = \Sigma_i SN_{i3} q_i^{(3)} + \Sigma_i SN_{i5} q_i^{(5)} + \Sigma_i SN_{i2} q_i^{(2)} + \Sigma_i SN_{i6} qs_i^{(2)} \quad 1$$

(d)

$$a = \Sigma_i SN_{i3} a^* + \Sigma_i SN_{i5} (p_i^q + q_i^{(5)}) + \Sigma_i SN_{i2} (p_i^q + q_i^{(2)}) + \Sigma_i SN_{i6} (p_i^q + qs_i^{(2)}) \quad 1$$

16. *Balance of Trade Condition*

$$\pi = SXe + SMm \quad 1$$

17. *Balance of Trade Identities*

(a) Total Export Value

$$e = \Sigma_i V_i (p_{i1} + cd_{i1}) \quad 1$$

(b) Total Import Value

$$m = \Sigma_i M_i (p_{i2} + q_{i1}) \quad 1$$

(c) Total Export Volume

$$e_R = \Sigma_i V_i cd_{i1} \quad 1$$

(d) Total Import Volume

$$m_R = \Sigma_i M_i q_{i1} \qquad 1$$

18. *Composite Price Variables*

(a) Price Level Determination

$$p^q = ms - a_R \qquad 1$$

(b) Price Deflator for GDP

$$p^x = \Sigma_i K_i p_i^x \qquad 1$$

(c) Price Deflator for Total Absorption

$$p^q = \Sigma_i W_i p_i^q \qquad 1$$

(d) Price Deflator for Absorption of i

$$p_i^q = \sum_{s=1}^{2} A_{is} p_{is} \qquad g$$

(e) Price Deflator for Output of i

$$p_i^x = \sum_{d=1}^{2} J_{id} p_{id} \qquad g$$

Total Number of Equations: 2gh + 19g + 6h + 13

Endogenous Variables (Percentage Change)

a	Nominal absorption	1
a^*	Household nominal absorption	1
c_i	Output of commodity i	g
c_{ij}	Output of commodity i by sector j	gh
cd_{id}	Supply of commodity i to destination d	2g
e	Export Value	1
e_R	Export Volume	1
gdp_r	Real gdp	1

gdp	Nominal gdp	1
m	Import value	1
m_R	Import volume	1
p_{is}^{e}	Foreign currency price of export i, s = 1, China	g
p_{vj}^{P}	Return to primary factor v in industry i	2h + 1
p_i^{m}	Foreign currency price of import i	g
p_q	Composite price for absorption	1
p_i^{q}	Price for absorption of i	g
p_{ik}	Price of i in 1, export; 2, import; 3, domestic	3g
p_i^{x}	Price for production of i (composite of domestic and export)	g
p^{x}	Aggregate price of output (gdp defl.)	1
q_i	Total absorption of i	g
$q_{ij}^{(1)}$	Intermediate use of i by industry j	gh
$q_i^{(2)}, qs_i^{(2)}$	Fixed and stock investment demands for i	2g
$q_i^{(3)}$	Household demand for i	g
$q_i^{(4)}$	Export demand for i from China	g
$qw_i^{(4)}$	World demand for good i	g
$q_i^{(5)}$	Government demand for i	g
q_{is}	Demand for i from source s = 1, import; 2, domestic	2g
q_{vj}^{P}	Demand for primary factor v by industry j (v=1, labour; 2, capital; 3, land)	3h
x_j	Output level of industry j	h
π	Balance of trade as a share of gdp	1
ϕ_2	Secondary market exchange rate	1
Total Number of Endogenous Variables		*2gh+19g+6h+13*

Exogenous Variables (Percentage Change)

a_R	Real absorption
ac_i	Output i augmenting technical change
af	Neutral factor augmenting technical change
af_v	Factor v augmenting technical change
af_{vj}	Factor v augmenting technical change in sector j
ah	Factor and input augmenting technical change
ah_j	Factor and input augmenting technical change in sector j

ai_j Commodity j augmenting technical change

ai_{jh} Commodity j augmenting technical change in sector h

ff_i Shifter for fixed investment demand for c

fs_i Shifter for stocks investment demand for i

gd_i Shifter for government demand for i

k_j Capital stock in industry j

l_j Land use by industry j

ms Money supply

P_{is}^{e} Foreign currency price of good i, s=2, R.O.W

q_1^P Total labour force

rr_i Foreign exchange retention rate for exports of i

t_i Power of the tariff on imports of i

v_i Power of the export tax on exports of i (1 - nominal export tax)

ϕ_1 Official exchange rate (Yuan/US$)

Value Share Coefficients

A_{is} Share of absorption of i derived from source s

$B_{ij}^{(1)}$ Share of intermediate use by industry j in total absorption of i

$B_i^{(2)}$ Share of investment in total absorption of commodity i

$BS_i^{(2)}$ Share of stock demand in total absorption of commodity i

$B_i^{(3)}$ Share of household consumption in total absorption of commodity i

$B_i^{(5)}$ Share of government in total absorption of i

ES_{is} Share of China and R.O.W. in world export markets for i

FES_1	Share of export revenue obtained from sales at official exchange rate $((1-R_o)\phi_1)/(R_o\phi_2 + (1-R_o)\phi_1)$, where R_o = base period retention rate
$G_i^{(2)}$	Share of commodity i fixed investment in GDP
$GS_i^{(2)}$	Share of commodity i stock investment in GDP
$G_i^{(3)}$	Share of commodity i household demand in GDP
$G_i^{(4)}$	Share of commodity i export demand in GDP
$G_i^{(5)}$	Share of commodity i government demand in GDP
$G_i^{(6)}$	Share of commodity i import demand in GDP
GR_{ij}	Share of commodity i in total output value of activity j
$H_{ij}^{(1)}$	Share of intermediate good i in total costs of industry j
H_{vj}^{p}	Share of primary factor v in total costs of industry j
J_{id}	Share of good i production to destination 1: export; 2, domestic
K_i	Share of sector i in total value added
L_j	Share of industry j in total employment
M_i	Share of i in total imports
OA_{ij}	Share of activity j in total output of commodity i
RC	Conversion factor from proportional change in retention rate (R) to change in (1-R), i.e., $(-R_o/(1 - R_o))$
S_{vj}^{p}	Share of primary factor v in primary factor inputs of j
SM	Imports as a share of nominal GDP
SN_{ij}	Share of end-use demand j for commodity i in final absorption
SX	Exports as a share of nominal GDP
V_i	Share of i in total exports
W_i	Share of good i in total absorption

Elasticity Parameters

β_i	Global elasticity of excess demand for good i
E_i	Elasticity of import supply for good i to China
ϵ_i	Household expenditure elasticity for good i
η_{ij}	Price elasticity of household demand for good i with respect to price j
σ_i^c	Elasticity of transformation between commodity outputs of sector i
σ_i^m	Elasticity of substitution between import and domestic products of good i
σ_i^p	Elasticity of substitution between primary factor inputs in sector i
σ_i^T	Elasticity of transformation between domestic and export production of good i
σ_i^w	Elasticity of substitution between Chinese and R.O.W. products in world market for i

Figure 3.1. **Implications of Foreign Exchange Overvaluation**

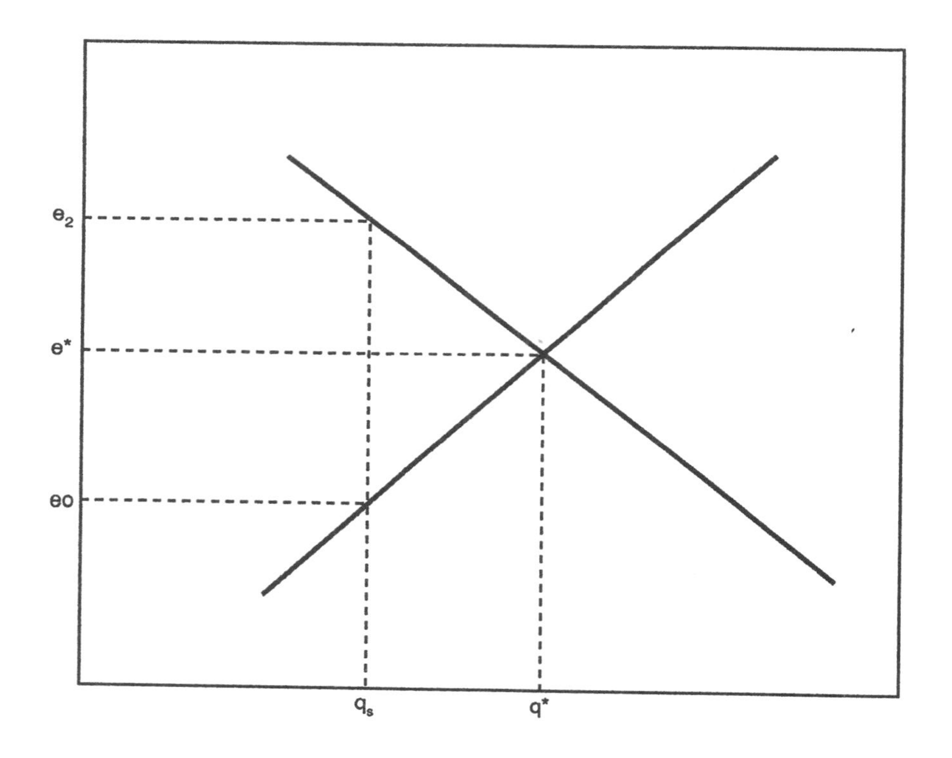

Appendix 3.1

Construction of the Input-Output Table for the China Agriculture in General Equilibrium Model

The input-output table for this model needed to provide a good deal of disaggregation of the agricultural sector while providing enough detail of the non-agricultural sector to allow the agricultural/non-agricultural sector linkages to be explored. Unfortunately, no existing table provided the required detailed information in both of these areas. The required table was constructed by incorporating information from the World Bank (1985a) table of the Chinese economy; the agricultural sector table constructed by Chen, Mao and Xue (1986) for the crops component of the agricultural sector; and information on the livestock industries obtained primarily from World Bank studies (1985c, 1987).

Based on the theory of two-tier pricing developed by Sicular (1988), Wu and Zhao (1987) and Byrd (1987), the table required for the analysis needed to be based on secondary market prices rather than the official prices in which the input-output tables were initially reported.

The input-output table at secondary market prices prepared by Thompson (1990, 1991) using the World Bank table and additional information on relationships between plan and market prices was the logical beginning point for the construction of the overall table. Once a satisfactory representation of the agricultural sector had been constructed, a more detailed representation of the agricultural sector was obtained by expanding the agricultural sector entries in the Thompson table to provide much more detailed information on production relationships in Chinese agriculture.

Given the very limited treatment of the livestock industries in the Chen *et al.* agricultural table, it was necessary to construct an input-output framework for the livestock sectors to obtain a complete representation of the Chinese agricultural economy. For the livestock sectors, as distinct from the crop sectors, the conventional input-output convention of treating each commodity as being produced by a separate activity was followed. This treatment is attractive because it allows for marked differences in the input mixes, and particularly in the feed-use intensity of each activity.

The first step in this process was to obtain estimates of gross output value at market prices for each livestock commodity using food balance sheet and market price data (World Bank, 1985c).

All of the input-output tables available for the Chinese economy and for the agricultural sector contained the same number of sectors as commodities, resulting in a square matrix of intermediate product flows. For the new model, however, there seemed good reasons to deviate from this pattern. Given the relative ease with which resources can be shifted from one crop to another in the crops sector, and the difficulty of obtaining reliable information on the extent to which specific inputs (eg. fertilizer, labour) are applied to one crop rather than another, it was decided to construct a composite crops activity which would produce multiple commodity outputs. This implies an input-output matrix with more (commodity) rows than (activity) columns and requires the construction of a Make matrix mapping from sectoral activity levels to commodity output levels.

Given the emphasis of the new model on the major agricultural activities and commodities in China, the wool sector identified in the special purpose Thompson (1990) table was merged with the overall animal husbandry sector since wool accounts for only a very small share of the value of agricultural output. The separate cotton sector identified in the Thompson table was also merged with the aggregate crops sector although cotton was retained as a separate commodity in the new model.

Prior to incorporating the detailed crop commodity and activity information from the Chen *et al.* table, the prices for all of these flows were converted from the official prices used in the table to estimated secondary market prices. This adjustment was based on the extensive price comparisons provided in studies by the World Bank (1985c) and by Lardy (1983) together with scattered information from unpublished sources. The price adjustment factors finally applied were 1.85 for rice, 1.9 for wheat, 1.96 for other grains, 1.63 for soybeans and other oil crops, and 1.5 for all other crops.

Following these adjustments, the basic procedure adopted in the construction of the new table was to use the information contained in the Chen *et al.*, (1986) table and in the constructed livestock activities to split the composite "Crops" and "Livestock" commodities contained in the Thompson table into the much more disaggregated commodity groupings required for the new table. This allocation was done in such a way that total crop output (and cost) levels corresponded to the totals obtained from the Thompson table. This disaggregation was required for three distinct sections of the table: (i) the intermediate use of crop/livestock commodities by these sectors; (ii) the use of crop/livestock commodities by other sectors and in final demand, and (iii) the intermediate use of other commodities and of primary factors by the crop and livestock sectors.

Information on the intermediate use of agricultural commodities by the crops sector was obtained from the Chen *et al.* table and aggregated into a single crops sector from the range of distinct crops sectors contained in that table. Feed inputs of particular agricultural commodities into livestock sectors were initially allocated using detailed information on the consumption of high-quality feed by livestock type (World Bank, 1987, p. 150) and on the commodity composition of high-quality feeds (Chen *et al.*, 1986). Inputs of other, less important, inputs into the livestock activities (eg.

electricity, coal and chemicals) were simply pro-rated from the total entries given for "livestock" in the Thompson table on the basis of the gross output value of the individual livestock activities.

The relatively minor entries for intermediate use of crop and livestock commodities by non-agricultural sectors were generally obtained by subdividing total intermediate use of crops in each sector on the basis of the shares of each of the crops in total crop output. Exceptions to this general approach were made in the textiles sector and the food-processing sector where more detailed information on the composition of intermediate use of crops was available from the Chen *et al.* table. One other exception was made in the chemical industry where the use of cotton in the Thompson table was held fixed and only the (quite small) use of non-cotton crop inputs was allocated using the crop output rule.

Final demands for crops were allocated initially using the proportions for components of final demands, and for competing imports, obtained from the Chen *et al.* table. The gross output value for each of the livestock sectors was inferred using the quantity estimates for 1982 provided in the World Bank Food Balance Sheets for 1982 (World Bank, 1985c) valued on the basis of estimates of market prices obtained from the same report.

Intermediate use of non-agricultural commodities in the crops sector was obtained directly from the Thompson table. Intermediate use of non-agricultural commodities by total livestock sector was generally split along the rows on the basis of the gross output value of each of the new livestock sectors. Use of primary factors in the crops sector was obtained from the Thompson table. Factor intensities for the individual livestock sectors were estimated using the detailed activity budgets for pig and poultry activities included in the World Bank livestock sector study (1987, p. 189).

Within the adjustment process it was necessary to make some careful distinctions because of the different procedures adopted by various authors. In particular, the Chen *et al.* agricultural table identified a much smaller proportion of agricultural output as being processed by the food-processing sector than did the World Bank table. With a view to representing the food-processing sector explicitly, the World Bank table's split of crop and livestock outputs between food processing and direct consumption was utilized. The World Bank table, by contrast, did not explicitly identify any use of animal power as an input into the crops sector. This important output of the cattle (and other large animal) sector was made explicit without changing the overall characteristics of the table by adding animal power to the reported gross output of the crops sector and incorporating a corresponding additional source of intermediate demand.

The incorporation of information from different sources as described above inevitably resulted in (typically relatively small) violations of the consistency properties of the input-output table. The RAS procedure was used initially to ensure that the three sections of the table where major changes had been made continued to add up to the totals in the Thompson table: *(i)* the columns describing the new livestock activities, *(ii)* the rows describing the uses of the crop commodities, and *(iii)* the rows describing the uses of the livestock commodities.

The final table on which the model is based is presented in Appendix Table A.3.1. All entries in the table are in billions of yuan at domestic prices.

Table A3.1. **Input-output Table for the China Agriculture in General Equilibrium Model**

SECTORS	Crops	Cattle	Pigs	Poultry	Sheep	Fish	An. Husb.	Metals	Elec.
COMMODITIES									
Rice	4.93	0.93	4.87	1.45	0.18	1.57	9.00	0.00	0.00
Wheat	5.56	0.45	2.35	0.70	0.09	0.76	4.35	0.00	0.00
Tuber crops	1.78	0.22	1.15	0.34	0.04	0.37	2.12	0.00	0.00
Other grains	2.68	1.76	9.21	2.75	0.35	2.97	17.04	0.00	0.00
Soybeans & oil-crops	2.29	0.36	1.89	0.56	0.07	0.61	3.49	0.00	0.00
Cotton & hemp crops	0.00	0.00	0.00	0.00	0.00	0.00	0.00	0.00	0.00
Sugar & tobacco	0.07	0.00	0.00	0.00	0.00	0.00	0.00	0.00	0.00
Tea, fruit, vegetables	0.00	0.00	0.00	0.00	0.00	0.00	0.00	0.00	0.00
Other crops	1.35	0.00	0.00	0.00	0.00	0.00	0.00	0.00	0.00
Forestry	0.55	0.00	0.00	0.00	0.00	0.00	0.00	0.00	0.00
CROPS	*19.21*	*3.72*	*19.47*	*5.80*	*0.73*	*6.28*	*36.00*	*0.00*	*0.00*
Cattle	13.30	0.27	0.00	0.00	0.00	0.00	0.27	0.00	0.00
Pigs	0.00	0.00	0.73	0.00	0.00	0.00	0.73	0.00	0.00
Poultry	0.00	0.00	0.00	0.25	0.00	0.00	0.25	0.00	0.00
Sheep	0.00	0.00	0.00	0.00	0.07	0.00	0.07	0.00	0.00
Fisheries	0.00	0.00	0.00	0.00	0.00	0.18	0.18	0.00	0.00
ANIM. HUSBANDRY	*13.30*	*0.27*	*0.73*	*0.25*	*0.07*	*0.18*	*1.50*	*0.00*	*0.00*
Metallurgy	0.30	0.00	0.01	0.00	0.00	0.00	0.02	17.71	0.11
Electricity	1.41	0.06	0.16	0.06	0.02	0.04	0.34	2.81	2.87
Coal	1.02	0.04	0.12	0.04	0.01	0.03	0.24	3.00	4.34
Oil-mining	0.00	0.00	0.00	0.00	0.00	0.00	0.00	1.24	3.40
Refining	8.22	0.35	0.94	0.32	0.10	0.24	1.95	1.68	2.16
Chemicals	29.00	0.00	0.01	0.00	0.00	0.00	0.02	0.60	0.02
Chemical fibre	0.00	0.00	0.00	0.00	0.00	0.00	0.00	0.00	0.00
Machinery	2.10	0.03	0.07	0.02	0.01	0.02	0.14	3.92	0.01
Building materials	0.22	0.01	0.04	0.01	0.00	0.01	0.08	0.15	0.02
Wood	0.15	0.01	0.04	0.01	0.00	0.01	0.08	0.38	0.02
Food processing	0.84	0.05	0.25	0.08	0.01	0.08	0.47	0.56	0.01
Textiles	0.28	0.01	0.03	0.01	0.00	0.01	0.07	1.04	0.01
Apparel	0.12	0.01	0.01	0.00	0.00	0.00	0.03	1.01	0.00
Paper	0.10	0.00	0.00	0.00	0.00	0.00	0.01	0.53	0.01
Misc. mfg.	0.13	0.01	0.03	0.01	0.00	0.01	0.07	0.52	0.01
Construction	0.73	0.00	0.00	0.00	0.00	0.00	0.00	2.61	0.00
Freight transport	1.01	0.01	0.03	0.01	0.00	0.01	0.07	3.20	0.12
Passenger transport	0.01	0.00	0.00	0.00	0.00	0.00	0.01	0.19	0.03
Commerce	1.12	0.01	0.03	0.01	0.00	0.01	0.06	1.58	0.10
Misc. services	0.04	0.00	0.01	0.00	0.00	0.00	0.02	0.25	0.01
Education and health	0.00	0.00	0.00	0.00	0.00	0.00	0.00	0.00	0.00
Pub. adm. & defence	0.00	0.00	0.00	0.00	0.00	0.00	0.00	0.00	0.00
Housing	0.00	0.00	0.00	0.00	0.00	0.00	0.00	0.00	0.00
INTERMEDIATE	*79.31*	*4.61*	*22.00*	*6.66*	*0.97*	*6.94*	*41.18*	*42.98*	*13.25*
Labour value added	137.64	3.59	9.72	3.35	0.99	2.44	20.09	3.90	1.09
Capital value added	28.00	0.73	1.98	0.68	0.20	0.50	4.09	26.28	4.48
Land value added	67.65	5.88	1.53	0.04	1.14	1.29	9.88	0.00	0.00
GROSS OUTPUT VALUE	*312.60*	*14.82*	*35.23*	*10.73*	*3.30*	*11.16*	*75.24*	*73.16*	*18.81*

Table A3.1. (contd 1)

SECTORS	Coal	Mining	Refi-ning	Chemicals	Chem. Fibre	Machi-nery	Bld. Mat.	Wood	Food	Textl
COMMODITIES										
Rice	0.14	0.00	0.00	1.51	0.00	0.00	0.71	1.19	22.42	0.00
Wheat	0.08	0.00	0.00	0.91	0.00	0.00	0.43	0.72	15.41	0.12
Tuber crops	0.02	0.00	0.00	0.21	0.00	0.00	0.10	0.16	0.13	0.00
Other grains	0.10	0.00	0.00	1.02	0.00	0.00	0.49	0.81	0.82	0.01
Soybeans & oil-crops	0.04	0.00	0.00	0.48	0.00	0.00	0.22	0.37	3.00	0.00
Cotton & hemp crops	0.01	0.00	0.00	0.45	0.00	0.00	0.05	0.09	0.00	17.16
Sugar & tobacco	0.01	0.00	0.00	0.10	0.00	0.00	0.05	0.08	3.32	0.00
Tea, fruit, vegetables	0.06	0.00	0.00	0.63	0.00	0.00	0.30	0.50	0.94	0.00
Other crops	0.01	0.00	0.00	0.15	0.00	0.00	0.07	0.12	0.41	0.00
Forestry	0.05	0.00	0.00	0.58	0.00	0.00	0.27	0.45	2.95	0.00
CROPS	*0.53*	*0.00*	*0.00*	*6.04*	*0.00*	*0.00*	*2.70*	*4.50*	*49.39*	*17.29*
Cattle	0.00	0.00	0.00	0.00	0.00	0.00	0.00	0.00	0.26	0.40
Pigs	0.00	0.00	0.00	0.05	0.00	0.01	0.00	0.00	9.85	0.66
Poultry	0.00	0.00	0.00	0.02	0.00	0.00	0.00	0.00	3.06	0.00
Sheep	0.00	0.00	0.00	0.00	0.00	0.00	0.00	0.00	0.50	1.88
Fisheries	0.00	0.00	0.00	0.02	0.00	0.00	0.00	0.00	3.29	0.00
ANIM. HUSBANDRY	*0.00*	*0.00*	*0.00*	*0.09*	*0.00*	*0.02*	*0.00*	*0.00*	*16.96*	*2.93*
Metallurgy	0.72	0.24	0.00	1.44	0.00	39.04	0.64	0.16	0.08	0.02
Electricity	1.22	0.35	0.17	3.36	0.05	1.40	0.71	0.14	0.44	0.94
Coal	1.65	0.02	0.00	2.07	0.00	0.78	2.49	0.15	0.65	0.70
Oil-mining	0.00	2.24	33.08	3.00	0.00	0.64	0.28	0.04	0.16	0.72
Refining	0.36	0.54	0.60	7.02	0.16	2.46	0.48	0.27	1.17	2.00
Chemicals	0.50	0.80	0.20	31.86	0.02	5.20	1.00	0.50	5.60	3.58
Chemical fibre	0.00	0.00	0.00	0.00	0.00	0.00	0.00	0.00	0.00	11.76
Machinery	0.98	0.70	0.14	2.10	0.01	41.22	1.12	0.35	0.14	2.41
Building materials	0.08	0.15	0.02	0.30	0.00	0.45	2.27	0.15	0.08	0.07
Wood	0.90	0.02	0.02	0.08	0.00	0.60	0.60	2.07	0.02	0.28
Food processing	0.14	0.14	0.01	3.50	0.00	0.56	0.14	0.07	5.96	0.03
Textiles	0.50	0.70	0.03	1.47	0.01	1.00	0.80	0.14	0.21	31.92
Apparel	0.30	0.10	0.01	0.24	0.00	0.77	0.35	0.07	0.07	0.05
Paper	0.02	0.11	0.01	0.70	0.02	0.55	0.44	0.11	0.15	0.53
Misc. mfg	0.26	0.13	0.01	0.59	0.07	0.85	0.26	0.09	0.01	1.21
Construction	2.32	0.00	0.00	1.09	0.00	2.18	0.87	0.00	0.00	0.00
Freight transport	0.41	0.41	0.11	1.96	0.14	4.66	1.22	0.45	1.11	0.00
Passenger transport	0.06	0.06	0.03	0.32	0.00	0.52	0.06	0.06	0.38	0.24
Commerce	0.40	0.57	0.02	2.90	0.02	3.52	2.06	0.24	0.79	2.06
Misc. services	0.04	0.03	0.01	0.20	0.00	0.34	0.04	0.02	0.10	0.10
Education & health	0.00	0.00	0.00	0.00	0.03	0.00	0.00	0.00	0.00	0.00
Pub. adm. & defence	0.00	0.00	0.00	0.00	0.00	0.00	0.00	0.00	0.00	0.00
Housing	0.00	0.00	0.00	0.00	0.00	0.00	0.00	0.00	0.00	0.00
INTERMEDIATE	*11.38*	*7.30*	*34.46*	*70.32*	*0.54*	*106.75*	*18.52*	*9.58*	*83.47*	*78.84*
Labour value added	5.78	0.73	0.10	4.52	0.56	14.27	4.47	2.68	3.73	4.85
Capital value added	7.82	43.57	10.29	48.36	2.93	37.32	11.82	4.22	11.20	23.26
Land value added	0.00	0.00	0.00	0.00	0.00	0.00	0.00	0.00	0.00	0.00
GROSS OUTPUT VALUE	*24.98*	*51.60*	*44.85*	*123.20*	*4.02*	*158.36*	*34.82*	*16.49*	*98.40*	*106.94*

Table A3.1. (contd 2)

SECTORS	Apparel	Paper	Misc. Mfg	Constr.	Frt Tpt	Pas. Tpt
COMMODITIES						
Rice	0.24	1.24	1.04	1.67	0.00	0.00
Wheat	0.14	0.75	0.63	1.01	0.00	0.00
Tuber crops	0.03	0.17	0.14	0.23	0.00	0.00
Other grains	0.16	0.84	0.71	1.13	0.00	0.00
Soybeans & oil-crops	0.07	0.39	0.33	0.52	0.00	0.00
Cotton & hemp crops	0.02	0.09	0.08	0.12	0.00	0.00
Sugar & tobacco	0.02	0.08	0.07	0.11	0.00	0.00
Tea, fruit, vegetables	0.10	0.52	0.43	0.70	0.00	0.00
Other crops	0.02	0.13	0.11	0.17	0.00	0.00
Forestry	0.09	0.47	0.40	0.64	0.00	0.00
CROPS	*0.89*	*4.68*	*3.93*	*6.30*	*0.00*	*0.00*
Cattle	0.00	0.00	0.00	0.00	0.00	0.00
Pigs	0.02	0.00	0.00	0.00	0.00	0.00
Poultry	0.01	0.00	0.00	0.00	0.00	0.00
Sheep	0.00	0.00	0.12	0.00	0.00	0.00
Fisheries	0.01	0.00	0.00	0.00	0.00	0.00
ANIM. HUSBANDRY	*0.03*	*0.00*	*0.12*	*0.00*	*0.00*	*0.00*
Metallurgy	0.13	0.00	1.28	10.37	0.80	0.00
Electricity	0.05	0.43	0.65	0.17	0.09	0.02
Coal	0.08	0.33	0.45	0.24	0.89	0.14
Oil-mining	0.04	0.04	0.32	0.00	0.00	0.00
Refining	0.12	0.39	0.66	1.35	4.77	3.00
Chemicals	1.22	3.00	1.20	4.80	0.30	1.20
Chemical fibre	0.00	0.00	0.00	0.00	0.00	0.00
Machinery	0.18	0.28	0.42	13.58	1.26	1.44
Building materials	0.00	0.00	0.15	29.18	0.00	0.00
Wood	0.03	1.95	0.38	3.75	0.00	0.00
Food processing	1.06	0.07	0.70	0.14	0.14	0.00
Textiles	35.00	0.40	0.98	0.33	0.04	0.00
Apparel	2.33	0.00	0.27	1.18	0.16	0.00
Paper	0.13	5.58	0.44	0.50	0.22	0.00
Misc. mfg	0.23	0.26	3.58	1.82	0.00	0.00
Construction	0.00	0.00	0.15	5.80	5.80	0.00
Freight transport	0.84	0.54	0.95	2.67	0.54	0.08
Passenger transport	0.12	0.06	0.06	0.20	0.06	0.00
Commerce	0.24	0.54	1.49	1.77	0.74	0.11
Misc. services	0.03	0.03	0.03	0.08	0.06	0.00
Education & health	0.00	0.00	0.00	0.00	0.00	0.00
Pub. adm. & defence	0.00	0.00	0.00	0.00	0.00	0.00
Housing	0.00	0.00	0.00	0.00	0.00	0.00
INTERMEDIATE	*42.76*	*18.58*	*18.19*	*84.23*	*15.87*	*5.99*
Labour value added	4.06	2.14	2.63	11.09	6.77	1.25
Capital value added	2.25	1.20	4.08	13.58	8.86	1.05
Land value added	0.00	0.00	0.00	0.00	0.00	0.00
GROSS OUTPUT VALUE	*49.06*	*21.92*	*24.90*	*108.90*	*31.49*	*8.29*

Table A3.1. (contd 3)

SECTORS	Comm.	Misc. services	Educ. & Health	R&D	Housing	Total Intermed.
COMMODITIES						
Rice	1.76	0.00	0.56	0.00	0.00	46.40
Wheat	1.07	0.00	0.34	0.00	0.00	31.52
Tuber crops	0.24	0.00	0.08	0.00	0.00	5.40
Other grains	1.20	0.00	0.38	0.00	0.00	27.39
Soybeans & oil-crops	0.55	0.00	0.18	0.00	0.00	11.95
Cotton & hemp crops	0.13	0.00	0.04	0.00	0.00	18.25
Sugar & tobacco	0.12	0.00	0.04	0.00	0.00	4.05
Tea, fruit, vegetables	0.74	0.00	0.23	0.00	0.00	5.14
Other crops	0.18	0.00	0.06	0.00	0.00	2.79
Forestry	0.67	0.00	0.21	0.00	0.00	7.34
CROPS	*6.66*	*0.00*	*2.11*	*0.00*	*0.00*	*160.23*
Cattle	0.04	0.00	0.00	0.00	0.00	14.27
Pigs	1.70	0.00	0.00	0.00	0.00	13.02
Poultry	0.53	0.00	0.00	0.00	0.00	3.87
Sheep	0.16	0.00	0.00	0.00	0.00	2.74
Fisheries	0.57	0.00	0.00	0.00	0.00	4.06
ANIM. HUSBANDRY	*3.00*	*0.00*	*0.00*	*0.00*	*0.00*	*37.95*
Metallurgy	0.00	0.00	0.00	0.00	0.00	73.06
Electricity	0.47	0.20	0.30	0.00	0.00	18.59
Coal	0.32	0.11	0.54	0.00	0.00	20.18
Oil-mining	0.00	0.00	0.00	0.00	0.00	45.20
Refining	0.00	0.00	0.06	0.00	0.00	39.42
Chemicals	3.80	0.20	14.52	0.00	0.20	109.34
Chemical fibre	0.00	0.00	0.00	0.00	0.00	11.76
Machinery	6.02	0.21	2.24	0.00	0.21	81.19
Building materials	0.00	0.00	0.00	0.00	0.60	33.95
Wood	0.00	0.00	0.00	0.00	0.38	11.67
Food processing	5.60	0.28	2.10	0.00	0.00	22.53
Textiles	1.56	0.20	2.30	0.00	0.00	78.99
Apparel	0.14	0.10	1.10	0.00	0.00	8.40
Paper	2.20	0.33	5.17	0.00	0.00	17.85
Misc. mfg	0.26	0.00	4.49	0.00	0.00	14.84
Construction	0.15	0.00	0.44	0.00	1.23	23.35
Freight transport	1.49	0.24	1.16	0.00	0.00	23.35
Passenger transport	0.13	0.00	0.00	0.00	0.00	2.63
Commerce	1.14	0.22	1.62	0.00	0.11	23.43
Misc. services	0.10	0.10	0.35	0.00	0.00	1.99
Education & health	0.00	0.00	0.00	0.00	0.00	0.03
Pub. adm. & defence	0.00	0.00	0.00	0.00	0.00	0.00
Housing	0.00	0.00	0.00	0.00	0.00	0.00
INTERMEDIATE	*33.03*	*2.19*	*38.49*	*0.00*	*2.73*	*859.93*
Labour value added	11.67	2.04	18.40	11.91	0.57	276.92
Capital value added	12.65	7.76	22.02	0.791	10.67	348.56
Land value added	0.00	0.00	0.00	0.00	0.00	77.53
GROSS OUTPUT VALUE	*57.35*	*11.99*	*78.91*	*12.70*	*13.97*	*1562.9*

Table A3.1. (end)

SECTORS	Consumption		Investment		Foreign trade		
	Hshld	Govt	Fixed	Stocks	Export	Import	**Gross Output**
COMMODITIES							
Rice	30.37	0.41	0.00	12.08	0.62	0.27	89.61
Wheat	22.74	0.25	0.00	7.97	0.00	9.92	52.56
Tuber crops	5.06	0.06	0.00	0.50	0.02	0.00	11.03
Other grains	24.74	0.28	0.00	1.60	0.42	0.96	53.46
Soybeans & oil-crops	10.53	0.13	0.00	6.00	0.60	0.31	28.89
Cotton & hemp crops	0.83	0.03	0.00	1.57	0.08	0.76	20.00
Sugar & tobacco	0.50	0.03	0.00	4.35	0.04	0.00	8.97
Tea, fruit, vegetables	18.53	0.17	0.00	1.72	1.45	0.01	27.00
Other crops	1.92	0.04	0.00	0.00	0.37	0.00	5.12
Forestry	4.76	0.16	6.51	-0.28	0.43	2.96	15.96
CROPS	*119.99*	*1.55*	*6.51*	*35.51*	*4.01*	*15.20*	*312.60*
Cattle	0.49	0.00	0.00	-0.05	0.12	0.00	14.82
Pigs	18.73	0.00	0.00	2.53	0.95	0.00	35.23
Poultry	5.82	0.00	0.00	0.79	0.25	0.00	10.73
Sheep	0.96	0.00	0.00	0.24	0.00	0.63	3.30
Fisheries	6.25	0.00	0.00	0.20	0.65	0.00	11.16
ANIM. HUSBANDRY	*32.25*	*0.00*	*0.00*	*4.47*	*1.20*	*0.63*	*75.24*
Metallurgy	0.00	0.00	0.00	2.40	2.80	5.10	73.16
Electricity	0.09	0.13	0.00	0.00	0.00	0.00	18.81
Coal	4.04	0.41	0.00	0.00	0.50	0.14	24.98
Oil-mining	0.08	0.00	0.00	0.00	6.32	0.00	51.60
Refining	0.99	0.87	0.00	0.00	3.63	0.06	44.85
Chemicals	11.94	2.00	0.00	3.12	5.92	9.12	123.20
Chemical fibre	0.00	0.00	0.00	0.35	0.00	8.09	4.02
Machinery	21.18	11.77	48.58	3.50	6.08	13.94	158.36
Building materials	0.00	0.30	0.00	0.30	0.29	0.02	34.82
Wood	4.97	0.75	0.00	0.30	0.57	1.77	16.49
Food processing	72.42	0.90	0.00	0.63	3.71	1.79	98.40
Textiles	20.59	0.52	0.00	3.74	6.00	2.90	106.94
Apparel	34.43	0.48	0.00	0.76	4.99	0.00	49.06
Paper	2.46	0.67	0.00	1.21	0.36	0.64	21.92
Misc. mfg	4.04	2.60	0.00	1.82	3.64	2.04	24.90
Construction	0.00	3.05	82.51	0.00	0.00	0.00	108.90
Freight transport	3.81	0.16	1.35	1.08	3.31	1.57	31.49
Passenger transport	3.10	2.56	0.00	0.00	0.00	0.00	8.29
Commerce	28.53	0.30	2.20	0.72	3.78	1.61	57.35
Misc. services	8.00	2.00	0.00	0.00	0.00	0.00	11.99
Education & health	3.60	75.28	0.00	0.00	0.00	0.00	78.91
Pub. adm. & defence	0.00	12.70	0.00	0.00	0.00	0.00	12.70
Housing	13.97	0.00	0.00	0.00	0.00	0.00	13.97
INTERMEDIATE	*390.48*	*118.99*	*141.15*	*59.91*	*57.10*	*64.61*	

Chapter 4

Analysing Impacts of Policy and Structural Shifts on the Agricultural Sector

4.1 Introduction

In this chapter we report experiments using the "China Agriculture in General Equilibrium Model" for three broad questions:

i) the extent of price distortions,

ii) macroeconomic policy impacts,

iii) growth and structural change effects.

These experiments were suggested by the discussion in Chapters 1 and 2 of policy developments in China and some of the empirical issues which were emerging. The first case applies the model to estimate an equilibrium exchange rate which can be used to decompose the extent of price distortion in China into effects of sector-specific policies and effects of economy-wide policies. In the other two cases, the model is used to simulate the effects of various policy changes or structural changes on the mix of output and the pattern of trade.

4.2 Protection Policy

As we explained in Chapter 2, the issue in this section is to derive estimates of domestic to border price ratios and then decompose these ratios into effects due to the exchange rate distortion and effects due to sector-specific policies. Since many different general types of policy distortion are involved, and many of these measures are non-transparent, the only available means for evaluating the magnitude of these distortions is the price comparison approach.

If the exchange rate were at its equilibrium level and there were no other trade distortions, the domestic price of a homogeneous good would equal the world price times the equilibrium exchange rate. A higher domestic price for a good implies that it is protected by some combination of exchange rate and trade policy distortions. A lower price implies that it is taxed by some combination of these measures.

An estimate of the equilibrium exchange rate which would arise in the absence of official exchange rate overvaluation can be obtained using the general equilibrium model developed for this study. Once an equilibrium exchange rate has been estimated, the tariff equivalent of the prevailing trade distortions can be calculated from the arbitrage condition:

$$p_d^i = e^*.p_{w^i}.(1+t^i) \qquad 4.1$$

where p_d^i is the domestic price of good i, e* is the equilibrium exchange rate, p_{wi} is the reference world price of good i, and t^i is the tariff (or export subsidy) equivalent of all of the trade and exchange rate distortions affecting good i. Since the same equilibrium exchange rate applies for both imports and exports, the trade distortions affecting imports and exports can be measured in the same way in this case.

While convenient in providing a single measure of protection, the single producer subsidy equivalent, or PSE, of the type defined above, and used in all previous studies of which we are aware (eg. Webb, 1989; Webb and Tuan, 1991; Gunasekera *et al.*, 1991) has the major disadvantage that it does not allow total protection to be decomposed into the effects of commodity-specific trade policy distortions and the economy-wide exchange rate distortions. Since the policy instruments which affect these distortions are administered by different institutions and can move independently, it seems highly desirable to be able to distinguish between the two types of distortion. The quantitative model developed for this study distinguishes between exchange rate distortions and commodity-specific trade distortions, and so requires estimates of the separate effects of these distortions.

For exports, the foreign exchange system acts like an export tax equal to the gap between the official and the "equilibrium" exchange rates. This tax is offset to some degree by the foreign exchange retention arrangements, which allow enterprises to retain a proportion of their foreign exchange earnings and to sell these earnings at the higher secondary market exchange rate. While the rate of retention varied between commodities, enterprises, regions and according to whether the product exported was within plan requirements or surplus to plan levels, an indicative benchmark level of foreign exchange retention during the 1980s was 25 per cent. On this basis, the exchange rate applying to exports was a weighted average of the official exchange rate and the secondary market rate, with weights of 0.75 and 0.25 respectively.

In the absence of commodity-specific trade distortions, the domestic price should equal the foreign price times the weighted average exchange rate for exports discussed above. A domestic price above this level requires some intervention such as an export subsidy or a quantitative export target which raises exports, and hence raises domestic prices. A domestic price below this level requires an export tax or a quantitive export control which depresses domestic prices, creating an effect equivalent to an export tax.

While some imports receive favoured treatment and are eligible for foreign exchange allocations at the official exchange rate, most marginal imports are purchased at the secondary market exchange rate. Thus, in the absence of any commodity-specific trade distortions, the domestic price of imports should equal their foreign price times the secondary market exchange rate. Domestic prices above this level are an indicator of commodity-specific protection superimposed upon the exchange rate distortions.

Arbitrage conditions similar to Equation 4.1 can be used to estimate the relevant commodity-specific rates of border protection or taxation on imports and exports. For any given pair of domestic and foreign prices of a comparable good, there will be two different protection rates — one being a tariff equivalent for imports and the other an export subsidy equivalent for exports. For these price comparisons to be meaningful, the domestic and internationally traded goods must be comparable in quality, and developers of reference price series typically go to a good deal of trouble to find data series which are sufficiently homogeneous as to allow a meaningful comparison.

If all of the domestic production of the good is identical with the foreign good, then the good will be either imported or exported, but not both, and only one of these trade distortions will be economically relevant. On the other hand, if the domestic product mix differs in some way such as the mix of product types, ease of transportation, or perceived quality, then two-way trade may be present, and both the tariff equivalent and the export subsidy equivalent may be economically relevant. Given the size of China, the transportation constraints and the variation in production, marketing and quality standards of crops, it seems likely that domestic and foreign commodities in aggregate will be imperfect substitutes even where commodities comparable with internationally traded commodities can be observed in coastal areas.

As noted above, the domestic prices needed to assess the impacts of policies are the market prices which affect decision making at the margin, rather than the largely *infra-marginal* prices received for production within quota or contract requirements. Unfortunately, the availability of consistent information on market, as distinct from plan, prices in China is extremely limited. Gunasekera *et al.* (1991) provide estimates for a very comprehensive set of commodities in 1986, while the World Bank (1990a, p. 31) study provides estimates for a few major commodities in 1987 and 1988. Using the techniques discussed above, estimates of total trade distortions and commodity-specific trade distortions for imports and exports of each commodity have been prepared and are presented in Table 4.1 for 1986.

The equilibrium exchange rate used in the calculations reported in this table is 4.31 yuan per dollar. This rate was estimated by calculating the increase in the official exchange rate which would be required to equalize the official and secondary market exchange rates in the model, and then expressing this exchange rate as a weighted average of the initial official and secondary market exchange rates. Given the model parameters and with the foreign exchange retention scheme for exports included in the analysis, the resulting weights were 0.51 on the official exchange rate and 0.49 on the secondary market exchange rate. These weights were preferred to the somewhat arbitrary adoption of one third and two thirds as weights by Gunasekera *et al.* (1991) and Yang and Tyers (1989). For 1986, the secondary market exchange rate averaged 5.2 per dollar (International Currency Analysis, 1989, p. 426), somewhat above the black market rate utilised by Gunasekera *et al.* (1991, p. 42)[1].

In nearly every case, whether exportable or importable, there are sector-specific policies which reduce domestic agricultural prices in China below their foreign equivalent. In the case of imports, the absolute extent of this bias would be reduced by foreign exchange reform and by the appreciation that would be induced by that reform, but nearly all the measures of distortions indicate that domestic prices remain below world prices. That is, foreign exchange reform and the subsequent appreciation of the secondary market rate would lower the domestic equivalent of world prices but not by so much that domestic prices would then exceed world prices.

For example, consider the case of an importable such as wheat. Its market price in 1986 was 517 yuan. The border price in $US was 152. Converting to yuan at the estimated equilibrium exchange rate estimated by the model of 4.31 the yuan price becomes 655, and so the extent of the distortion is (517/655)-1 which equals -0.21. Measured at the secondary market rate (5.2) which is relevant for imports, the distortion is even higher, and equal to -0.34. Thus the foreign exchange distortion partially offsets the effects of commodity-specific policies which act to tax agricultural producers.

In the case of exports, domestic prices are generally below world prices at the equilibrium exchange rate. That portion of the difference (taxation) which is contributed by commodity-specific policy measures is indicated by the last column of Table 4.1. In most cases, this constitutes the majority of the taxation. Exchange rate overvaluation contributes the remainder and raises total export tax rates for each commodity to those shown in column (3) of Table 4.1[2].

Further reforms in China which removed the sector-specific policies could therefore actually increase domestic prices of both importables and exportables. We discussed the implications of this result in Chapter 2, where we argued that the effect of a comprehensive trade policy reform on the agricultural sector in China would be a substantial decline in net imports. The net agricultural trade position would improve. The significance of this result is therefore that in the short run, the effects of reform at that time would have been to improve the degree of self sufficiency in the agricultural sector, not diminish it.

4.3 Macroeconomic Policy Impacts

A set of key results for three macroeconomic experiments are presented in Table 4.2. The effects of the shock on a range of macroeconomic variables is shown together with impacts on the output and trade levels for groups of aggregated sectors, and more disaggregated data are included in Table A4.1 at the end of this chapter.

The increase in domestic spending (absorption) results in a change in external balance with the volume of exports contracting and the volume of imports expanding. The 1 per cent increase in absorption results in a 6.7 per cent appreciation of the secondary market exchange rate (a negative number means the local price of foreign currency has fallen, that is, the exchange rate has appreciated). Thus the increase in demand for foreign and other goods in this model causes a fall in the price of imported goods. This is a counterintuitive result. It can be understood using the distinction of traded/non-traded goods of Salter (1959). The increase in demand for non-traded goods resulting from the increase in absorption requires an increase in the relative price of non-traded goods. Since the composite price of absorption (formed as a weighted average of imported and non-traded goods) is held constant as numeraire in this experiment, the required change in relative prices can only come about through a fall in the domestic prices of imported goods (export prices are determined to a large extent by the fixed nominal exchange rate and so as long as it stays fixed the nominal prices of exportables are roughly constant).

At the aggregate levels at which we report the results here there are only small changes in output in the various sectors. Overall, the output of the crop sector contracts. Strengthened import competition for some major crops, particularly wheat, through the fall in the price of imports, and low income elasticities for many major crops contribute to this result.

The increase in absorption increases the volume of imports of almost all commodities. The total increase in imports of 8.5 per cent is much larger than the increase in absorption because trade volumes are small relative to total absorption. Export volumes also decline across all the aggregate sectors in this analysis.

These results highlight the point made earlier: that macroeconomic management shocks will have differential impacts on various sectors, not only because of the effects of differences in income elasticities but also because of effects via the exchange market.

Another example of those effects is reported in the third column of the table which shows the results of a 10 per cent increase in money supply. As we stressed, this shock has real effects because of the rigidity of the nominal exchange rate.

A key implication of an increase in the money supply is a more than proportionate increase (depreciation) in the secondary market rate. This change can be decomposed into two parts. The first is an increase of 10 per cent to match the increase in the general price level. The price of exports is however constrained by the fixed nominal exchange rate. A rise in the level of domestic prices makes exporting less attractive, the supply of foreign exchange decreases, and this sets off a further rise (depreciation) in the secondary market rate. This second-round effect in the model is a real change in the secondary market rate of a further 6.7 percentage points.

The price of imported goods rises with the secondary market rate. In this experiment, the total increase in the price of absorption is constrained to be equal to 10 per cent. The price of non-traded goods also rises, but it must rise by less than 10 per cent since the price of imported goods has gone up by roughly 16.7 per cent.

These changes in relative prices lead both import and export volumes to fall overall. Real absorption is held constant in this experiment. Real incomes have however fallen because of the induced allocative inefficiencies in the economy. In other words, the price changes induced by this macro shock have an adverse effect on the performance of the economy. Maintaining real absorption while real income is falling requires more imports (an effect which is also included in the derivation of the equilibrium secondary market rate). As a consequence the import volume falls by less than exports. The effects on the trade balance are therefore adverse.

The effects of this shock on different sectors depends on their trade orientation. The output of export-orientated commodities (eg. fruit/vegetables or clothing) declines, since their relative prices have fallen, while the output of import competing commodities (like wheat) increases. The net effects in our aggregated sectors are shown in the table.

In the first experiment where absorption changed, income elasticities were important. In this case they are not, because spending is not changing. It is changes in relative prices which are driving the changes in output. The effect on output then also depends on supply and demand elasticities. Where supply elasticities are low and demand elasticities are high (eg. petroleum) there are small decreases in exports and large declines in imports. Where supply elasticities are high and demand elasticities low (eg. chemical fibres) there is a large reduction in exports and a small decline in imports.

The third experiment is an exchange rate depreciation. Compared to the money supply experiment, the signs on all the changes are reversed but otherwise the same in magnitude. The only other differences are in the secondary market exchange rate and the nominal price level. This is because a depreciation of the official rate is the same in real terms as holding the official rate constant while the price level falls by 10 per cent (the opposite effect to an increase in the money supply of 10 per cent). Here the depreciation of the official rate causes the secondary market rate to appreciate.

4.4 Growth and Structural Change

In this section we report some experiments designed to illustrate the effects of structural change in the model. The first column in Table 4.3 shows the so-called 'Dutch Disease' results, that is, an expansion in some part of the economy which has intersectoral effects. In this case the expansion is in the light industrial sector, rather than in the energy sector as occurred in the original Dutch Disease. This experiment is included here to capture some of the effects of the rural industrial boom in China. We model this sort of effect by increasing the efficiency with which all inputs (factors and intermediate goods) are used in the light industry sectors of textiles, clothing and miscellaneous manufacturing. In this experiment, the balance of trade in foreign currency as a share of base period GDP is held constant. In that case, the increase in income feeds back into increased absorption.

Absorption increases by 2.5 per cent and the price level falls by the same amount. That price fall, given the fixed exchange rate, raises the relative price of exports which are then more attractive. Export volume increases, the sectors contributing directly to that result being strongly export-orientated, but overall manufacturing exports increase as well. The secondary market rate also appreciates. Real wages rise consistent with these sectors, being relatively labour-intensive.

The effects on agricultural output are uneven, highlighting the value of the highly disaggregated modelling approach to these issues. For example, the output of crops declines, because resources are being bid away to the booming sectors and to the expanding non-traded sectors. The appreciation of the secondary market rate also lowers the prices of imports which adds to competition for local producers in some sectors. Finally, an important factor is the income elasticity of demand. The decline in output of the other crops sector is pronounced because of the low income elasticities of outputs like tubers. By contrast the output of animal products rises. This reflects a combination of a higher income elasticity and a stronger export orientation.

This is a particularly interesting experiment because the impacts on trade are dramatic. There are substantial increases in imports of grains and other crops. There are smaller increases in imports of animal products (alongside a fall in exports). These imports are paid for by the large increase in the exports of manufactures. Thus expanding exports of manufactures are paying for rising imports of grains and other crop products.

The second experiment in the table is that of a decline in the labour force with the size of the sectoral capital stocks held constant. This experiment is designed to examine a central feature of the development process (Leamer, 1987): that the capital to labour ratio increases. As a consequence the relatively labour-intensive sectors may grow more slowly or even contract. This long-term process involves the accumulation of capital which is difficult to simulate in the model used here. The model applies in the short run when the stock of capital is fixed in each industry. An approximation to the long-run situation is to vary the labour supply in order to raise the sectoral capital labour ratios, and then to see what sorts of pressures for adjustment emerge.

A change in the labour supply alone will generate large changes in income and spending, and the effects of that change would normally swamp the changes coming from the supply side. To try to limit the effects of spending changes and changes in the real exchange rate and to isolate the supply side effects, absorption was decreased (for a decrease in labour supply) so that capital inflow remained a constant proportion of GDP. If this was not assumed then income, spending or trade balance effects would have been less "neutral" and more difficult to disentangle from the supply side effects of interest here.

Output falls across the board, reflecting the drop in GDP, but all the sectoral output declines are less than 1 per cent since labour is the only input which is changing. Concentrating on the different rates of decline will highlight the implications for structural change. The results show larger declines in agriculture (more labour-intensive) than other sectors. Agricultural exports fall and imports rise. Self sufficiency therefore falls in agricultural products. Manufacturing exports fall but imports fall by a larger proportion.

In summary, these results point to a long-run decline in agricultural self sufficiency associated with continued growth in China. However, real world process of growth would involve not only differential rates of accumulation of the factors of production but also rising incomes. The intersectoral effects of that change would depend on the income elasticities of demand.

The third experiment reported in the table highlights the impact of those parameters. This experiment tries to capture the effects of growth by augmenting the productivity of all factors in all sectors (Hicks neutral technical change) and captures the spirit of traditional analyses of agriculture's decline in a growing economy (Anderson, 1987). This shock is probably best thought of as an annual productivity increment leading to continual changes in the variables at the rates reported in the table[3].

The first result is that the secondary market exchange rate continually appreciates at about 1.4 per cent a year. This reflects the high income elasticities for non-traded goods, so the price of non-traded goods must rise relative to the prices (determined by the secondary market rate) of importables.

Real GDP is growing at 1 per cent a year, so sectors with slower rates of growth of output will be falling significantly in this economy. Output effects depend on both income elasticities and on price effects via the changes in the secondary market exchange rate.

The animal husbandry, manufacturing and service sectors grow faster than 1 per cent. Since growth at 1 per cent implies constant actual (as distinct from effective) factor inputs, slower growth implies out-migration of factors. These results imply a movement of labour out of grains into the rest of the economy.

The trade impacts are determined by the interaction of the price effects and income elasticities. Income elasticities which are low for some agricultural products lead to increases in exports. Lower domestic prices and a fixed official exchange rate also make export production more attractive. Import volumes also rise, reflecting the competition from lower-priced importables as a result of the appreciating secondary market rate.

These two experiments have in common the result of the relative decline in share of output in the agricultural sector (especially the grain and crops sectors). Their trade implications are however different. The experiment in which factor intensity changes (reflecting the differential rate of factor accumulation in the process of growth) leads to large declines in agricultural self sufficiency. The neutral factor accumulation experiment produces results in the opposite direction, since import volumes rise but exports rise by more. However the orders of magnitude are smaller in the second experiment. This suggests that in the process of growth the supply side forces for adjustment will more than offset the smaller, positive effects of growth on trade positions associated with rising productivity and differential income elasticities.

4.5 Conclusions

In Chapter 2, we stressed that there was scope for substantial increases in productivity associated with further agricultural reforms in China. Moreover, as supported by more detailed evidence in this chapter, agricultural product prices were low (in the second half of the 1980s) compared to world prices. Price reforms would therefore have also added to growth in agricultural output. Reforms up to the mid-1980s had certainly generated an impressive growth in agricultural output. Those growth rates slumped in subsequent years, recovering again in the late 1980s and early 1990s. The recovery this time was (as we explain in Chapter 1) due to a combination of policy changes (higher prices) and good luck (the weather and its effect on yields). The contribution of price changes to output growth is not surprising, given the extent of the taxes on agricultural producers that we estimated applied in 1986. The benefits of the first round of reforms had continued to be taxed heavily through highly distorted prices. It took price changes in the late 1980s to kick along agricultural output again. Further institutional reforms are however also possible.

In the short run, these sorts of reforms would raise agricultural output growth and reduce reliance on imports. However in the longer run, there are powerful forces in the opposite direction. These were illustrated by the structural change experiments on the effects of a rural industrial boom, a change in factor endowments and growth in incomes. The former pair of changes were shown to have relatively large impacts on the degree of agricultural self-sufficiency compared to the impacts of income growth on demand (via different income elasticities).

Finally, the model results highlight the differential impacts of the management of macroeconomic policy in China. These occur not only because of the differential income elasticities of demand but also because of an important nominal rigidity in the Chinese economy, that is, the exchange rate. The model results indicate that small changes in macroeconomic variables can have substantial impacts on trade patterns in particular commodities. Given the pronounced macroeconomic instability which has occurred in this partially reformed economy, macroeconomic shocks seem likely to contribute substantially to fluctuations in China's agricultural trade.

Notes and References

1. In 1987, the official exchange rate was stable at 3.72 yuan per dollar and the average rate on the secondary markets rose to an estimated 5.9 per US dollar. In 1988, the official exchange rate again remained stable at 3.72 yuan per dollar while the secondary market rate rose to an average of 6.6 yuan per dollar.
2. In addition to the border distortions discussed above, attention needs to be paid to the impact of direct transfers from government to producers. This assistance takes a wide variety of forms including: the supply of inputs on concessional terms, interest rate subsidies, disaster relief, advance payments for crops, research and development assistance, differential treatment for taxation, and infrastructure development expenditure (Gunasekera *et al.*, p. 39). The dividing line between assistance which affects decisions at the margin and that which does not is very difficult to draw in the case of inputs, and we have made the simplifying assumption that all such measures affect decision-making at the margin. Our estimates of the magnitude of these input subsidies, expressed as a percentage of output value, were at most 4 per cent of the value of production.
3. This experiment also assumes that capital inflow is a constant proportion of GDP.

Table 4.1. **Agricultural Price Distortions, 1986**

	Market price (yuan/tonne)	Border price ($US/tonne)	Price Distortions: At eqm. exchange rate (4.31)	At secondary market rate (5.2)	At export rate[a] (3.89)
Beef	5 565	2 215	-0.42	-0.52	-0.35
Pork	3 256	1 605	-0.53	-0.61	-0.48
Mutton	3 949	1 412	-0.35	-0.46	-0.28
Poultry	3 862	1 032	-0.13	-0.28	-0.04
Eggs	3 013	840	-0.17	-0.31	-0.08
Milk	1 584	499	-0.26	-0.39	-0.18
Wheat	517	152	-0.21	-0.34	-0.12
Corn	422	114	-0.14	-0.29	-0.05
Other coarse grains	390	103	-0.12	-0.27	-0.03
Rice	501	197	-0.41	-0.51	-0.35
Soybeans	930	266	-0.19	-0.33	-0.10
Oilseeds	1 203	376	-0.26	-0.38	-0.18
Other meat	573	131	0.01	-0.16	0.12
Other oils	3 170	372	0.98	0.64	1.19
Cotton	3 216	770	-0.03	-0.20	0.07
Sugar	610	215	-0.34	-0.46	-0.27

a. The weighted average of 3.453 (0.75) and 5.2 (0.25) where the former is the official exchange rate.

Sources: Gunaskera *et al.*, and author calculations.

Table 4.2. **Effects of Shocks on Major Macroeconomic Variables**
(per cent change)

	Real absorption increase (1 %)	Money supply increase (10 %)	Official exchange rate devaluation (10 %)
Macro effects			
Secondary market exchange rate	-6.7	16.7	-6.7
Export volume	-2.8	-11.2	11.2
Import volume	8.5	-10.0	10.0
Real wage	1.6	-0.4	0.4
Consumer price	-1.0	10.0	0
Output levels			
Grains	-0.2	0.3	-0.3
Other crops	-0.3	-0.1	0.1
Animal husbandry	0.2	-0.4	0.4
Manufacturing	-0.01	-0.1	0.2
Services	0.5	-0.1	0.1
Export volumes			
Grains	-7.4	-13.5	13.5
Other crops	-7.1	-13.3	13.3
Animal husbandry	-7.5	-13.2	13.2
Manufacturing	-1.9	-10.8	10.8
Services	-5.2	-11.9	11.9
Import volumes			
Grains	10.1	-10.2	10.2
Other crops	7.3	-7.6	7.6
Animal husbandry	1.6	-1.7	1.7
Manufacturing	7.7	-9.9	9.9
Services	3.0	-3.5	3.5

Table 4.3. **Effects of Structural Changes**

(per cent change)

	"Dutch disease"[a]	Labour force decline (1 %)	Neutral technical change (1 %)
Macro effects			
Secondary market exchange rate	-9.1	0.25	-1.4
Export volume	12.9	-0.4	1.9
Import volume	10.7	-0.4	1.6
Real wage	1.0	1.9	-0.2
Consumer price	-2.5	0.4	-1.0
Output levels			
Grains	-0.3	-0.5	0.8
Other crops	-1.0	-0.6	1.0
Animal husbandry	0.2	-0.6	1.1
Manufacturing	2.1	-0.3	1.1
Services	1.3	-0.4	1.1
Export volumes			
Grains	-17.4	-4.0	3.5
Other crops	-16.6	-3.9	3.3
Animal husbandry	-17.4	-4.2	3.4
Manufacturing	20.7	-0.3	1.7
Services	11.6	-1.9	2.1
Import volumes			
Grains	17.1	1.1	0.7
Other crops	11.6	0.8	0.7
Animal husbandry	2.1	0.1	0.3
Manufacturing	7.6	-0.5	1.4
Services	4.8	0.03	0.5

a. 10 per cent increase in efficiency in use of all inputs in textiles, clothing and miscellaneous manufacturing.

Table A4.1. **Effects of Shocks on Major Macroeconomic Variables**
(per cent change)

	Real Absorption Increase (1%)	Money Supply Increase (10%)	Real Wage Increase (10%)	Official Exch. Rate Devaluation (10%)
Macro Effects				
Secondary market exchange rate	-6.7	16.7	-9.0	-6.7
Output volume	0	0	-1.6	0
Export volume	-2.8	-11.2	-6.1	11.2
Import volume	8.5	-10.0	11.8	10.0
Real wage*	1.6	-0.4	10	0.4
Consumer prices	-1.0	10	0	0
Employment levels	0	0	-4.0	0
Output Levels				
Rice	0.2	0.2	-1.3	-0.2
Wheat	-1.4	1.7	-4.9	-1.7
Tubers	0.02	-0.1	-1.0	0.1
Other grains	-0.1	0	-1.7	0
Oil crops	0.25	-0.2	-1.8	0.2
Cotton	-0.4	-0.1	-2.3	0.1
Sugar	0.7	-0.2	-0.9	0.2
Fruit/tea/vegetables	0.24	-0.7	-2.1	0.7
Other crops	-0.33	-0.9	-3.1	0.9
Forestry	-1.5	1.4	-5.2	-1.4
Crops	-0.2	0.2	-2.4	-0.2
Cattle	-0.2	0	-2.4	0
Pigs	0.5	-0.5	-1.8	0.5
Poultry	0.4	-0.4	-1.7	0.4
Sheep	-1.1	1.1	-4.0	-1.1
Fish	0.2	-0.8	-2.5	0.8
Metallurgy	-0.4	0.2	-1.5	-0.2
Electricity	0.1	0	-1.5	0
Coal	-0.1	-0.2	-1.8	0.2
Petroleum mining	-0.02	0	-0.1	0
Petroleum refining	-0.01	0	-0.2	0
Chemicals	-0.19	0.1	-0.9	-0.1
Chemical fibres	-0.7	0.7	-1.9	-0.7
Machinery	0.2	0.2	-1.8	-0.2
Building materials	-0.6	0.1	-0.6	-0.1
Wood	0.9	0.6	-3.3	-0.6
Food processing	0.60	0.3	-1.7	-0.3

Table A4.1. (contd 1)

	Real Absorption Increase (1%)	Money Supply Increase (10%)	Real Wage Increase (10%)	Official Exch. Rate Devaluation (10%)
Textiles	-0.1	-0.7	-1.3	0.7
Clothing	0.6	-1.1	-0.9	1.1
Paper	-0.1	0	-1.9	0
Misc. manufacturing	-0.7	-0.8	-3.5	0.8
Construction	0.8	0	-0.3	0
Freight transport	-0.6	-0.4	-3.1	0.4
Passenger transport	0.2	-0.1	-0.5	0.1
Commerce	0	-0.5	-2.5	0.5
Misc. services	0.6	0	-0.7	0
Education & health	1.0	0	0.0	0
Admin. & defence	1.0	0	0.0	0
Housing	0.2	0	-0.2	0
Exports				
Rice	-7.5	-13.5	-28.0	13.4
Wheat	-5.9	-15.5	-24.6	15.5
Tubers	-7.3	-13.6	-28.3	13.6
Other grains	-7.2	-13.7	-27.7	13.7
Oil crops	-7.5	-13.5	-27.5	13.5
Cotton	-6.9	-13.6	-27.1	13.6
Sugar	-7.9	-13.5	-28.4	13.5
Fruit/tea/vegetables	-7.5	-13.0	-27.2	13.0
Other crops	-6.9	-12.8	-26.3	12.8
Forestry	-5.7	-15.1	-24.2	15.1
Cattle	-6.7	-13.5	-18.2	13.5
Pigs	-7.5	-13.5	-30.2	13.4
Poultry	-7.3	-13.6	-30.8	13.5
Sheep	-1.9	-19.6	-13.3	19.6
Fish	-7.7	-12.7	-28.1	12.7
Metallurgy	2.9	-17.4	8.9	17.4
Electricity	-4.2	-8.2	-4.7	8.2
Coal	-6.3	-12.5	-20.4	12.6
Petroleum mining	0.1	-0.1	2.0	0.1
Petroleum refining	0.6	-0.2	16.1	0.2
Chemicals	1.1	-15.5	9.6	15.5
Chemical fibres	12.3	-33.0	18.0	33.0
Machinery	-1.7	-17.2	-3.4	17.3
Building materials	-11.5	-12.5	-22.2	12.5

Table A4.1. (end)

	Real Absorption Increase (1%)	Money Supply Increase (10%)	Real Wage Increase (10%)	Official Exch. Rate Devaluation (10%)
Wood	-2.5	-16.6	-14.0	16.6
Food processing	-7.5	-13.9	-19.5	13.9
Textiles	-3.6	-9.9	-4.1	9.9
Clothing	-4.0	-11.6	-9.0	11.6
Paper	-3.8	-15.2	-15.5	15.1
Misc. manufacturing	-3.3	-12.0	-10.6	12.0
Imports				
Rice	13.5	-13.8	27.4	13.8
Wheat	10.3	-10.2	20.0	10.2
Tubers	13.0	-13.7	27.7	13.8
Other grains	12.8	-13.4	26.5	13.5
Oil crops	13.7	-13.6	26.8	13.6
Cotton	12.3	-13.7	25.3	13.7
Sugar	14.4	-13.9	27.9	13.9
Fruit/tea/vegetables	14.0	-14.0	27.4	14.0
Other crops	13.0	-14.1	26.0	14.1
Forestry	10.1	-10.2	20.1	10.2
Cattle	12.4	-13.5	19.8	13.5
Pigs	14.1	-13.9	28.7	13.9
Poultry	13.9	-13.8	29.1	13.8
Sheep	8.2	-8.6	14.5	8.6
Fish	14.1	-14.4	27.4	14.3
Metallurgy	6.2	-10.2	4.4	10.2
Electricity	11.0	-16.9	12.9	16.9
Coal	12.4	-14.2	22.4	14.2
Petroleum mining	8.5	-21.6	10.5	21.6
Petroleum refining	8.2	-21.6	0.5	21.6
Chemicals	7.7	-11.3	4.6	11.3
Chemical fibres	0.5	-1.3	-1.0	1.3
Machinery	9.5	-10.3	11.8	10.3
Building materials	16.4	-14.3	24.7	14.3
Wood	8.9	-10.3	16.4	10.3
Food processing	14.3	-13.2	22.3	13.3
Textiles	11.2	-15.9	13.2	15.9
Clothing	12.7	-14.7	17.6	14.7
Paper	10.9	-12.4	19.1	12.4
Misc. manufacturing	10.3	-13.1	15.3	13.1

[a] Deflated by the absorption (consumption) price deflator.

Bibliography

ANDERSON, K., and R. TYERS (1987), "Economic Growth and Market Liberalization in China: Implications for Agricultural Trade", *The Developing Economies*, 25(2), 124-51.

ANDERSON, K. (1987), "On Why Agriculture Declines with Economic Growth", *Agricultural Economics*, 1, pp. 195-207.

ANDERSON, K (1990), *Changing Comparative Advantages in China: Effects on Food, Feed and Fibre Markets,* Development Centre Studies, OECD Development Centre, Paris.

ARMINGTON, P. (1969), "A Theory of Demand for Products Distinguished by Place of Production", *International Monetary Fund Staff Papers*, 16(2), 179-201.

BYRD, W. (1987), "The Impact of the Two-tier, Plan/Market System in Chinese Industry", *Journal of Comparative Economics*, 11(3), 295-308.

BYRD, W., and Q. LIN (1990), *China's Rural Industry*, Oxford University Press for the World Bank.

CAI FANG (1985), "Da-zhong chengshi nong-fu chanpin pifa shichang taolunhui jianjie", [A brief summary of the conference on Wholesale Markets for Agricultural Products in Large and Medium Cities], *Nongye Jingji Wenti,* [Problems of Agricultural Economics], No. 6, p. 49.

CCP CENTRAL COMMITTEE (1984), "Report on Creating a New Situation in Commune and Brigade-run Enterprises", in Zhongguo Nongye Nianjian Bianjibu, *Zhongguo Nongcun Fagui 1984* [China Rural Laws 1984], Beijing, Nongye Chubanshe, pp. 343-356.

CCP CENTRAL COMMITTEE (1985), "Ten Policies for Further Invigorating the Rural Economy", 1 January, in Zhongguo Nongye Nianjian Bianji Weiyuanhui, *Zhongguo Nongye Nianjian 1985* [China Agricultural Yearbook 1985], Beijing, Nongye Chubanshe, pp. 1-3.

CCP CENTRAL COMMITTEE (1991), "Decision on Agriculture and Rural Work", November, in *Summary of World Broadcasts,* Part 3, The Far East, FE/1268/C1/1-12.

CHAN, T. (1991), "No More Subsidies", *China Trade Report*, February.

CHEN, X., J. MAO, and X. XUE (1986), "The Input-output Table for Agricultural Sectors and its Application", Paper presented at the 8th International Conference on Input-Output Techniques, Sapporo, Japan, July 28-August 2.

CHEN CHUNLAI, A. WATSON, and C. FINDLAY (1991), "One State — Two Economies: Current Issues in China's Rural Industrialization", Chinese Economy Research Unit Working Paper No. 91/15, University of Adelaide.

CHOW, G. (1987), "Money and Price Level Determination in China", *Journal of Comparative Economics*, 11(3), 319-33.

CODSI, G., and K. PEARSON (1988), "GEMPACK: General Purpose Software for Applied General Equilibrium and Other Economic Modelers", *Computer Science in Economics and Management 1*, 189-207.

DERVIS, K., J. DE MELO, and S. ROBINSON (1981), "A General Equilibrium Analysis of Foreign Exchange Shortages in a Developing Country", *Economic Journal*, 91, 891-906.

DIXON, P., B. PARMENTER, J. SUTTON, and D. VINCENT (1982), *ORANI: A Multisectoral Model of the Australian Economy* (North-Holland, Amsterdam).

DONNITHORNE, A. (1967), *China's Economic System*, London, Allen and Unwin.

DU YING *et al.* (1989), "1988 nian yilai, ge di liangshi gouxiao tizhi gaige shiyan de qishi", [Lessons of the experiments in reform of the purchase and sales systems for grain in various localties since 1988], *Nongye Jingji Wenti*, [Problems in Agricultural Economics], No. 12, pp. 34-37.

FAN SHENGGEN (1991), "Effects of Technological Change and Institutional Reform on Production Growth in Chinese Agriculture", *American Journal of Agricultural Economics*, May.

FELTENSTEIN, A., and F. ZIBA (1987), "Fiscal Policy, Monetary Targets, and the Price Level in a Centrally Planned Economy: An Application to the Case of China", *Journal of Money, Credit and Banking*, 19(2), 137-56.

FENG GUOJUN (1987), "Hunan sheng nongcun jingji fazhan zijin gongxu zongliang de yuce yu duice", [An estimate of supply and demand for capital for rural economic development in Hunan Province and the appropriate policies to adopt], *Nongye Jingji Wenti*, [Problems in Agricultural Economics], No. 1, pp. 21-24.

FINDLAY, C., and A. WATSON (1991), "Surrounding the Cities from the Countryside: China's Rural Enterprises and their Implications for Growth, Trade and Economic Reform", paper prepared for the 19th Pacific Trade and Development (PAFTAD) Conference, on 'Economic Reforms and Internationalisation: China and the Pacific Region', Beijing, 27-30 May.

FINDLAY, C., ZHANG XIAOHE, and A. WATSON (1992), "Growth of Rural Enterprises, Urban-rural Relations and China's Foreign Trade", paper presented to the conference 'Trade, Investment and Economic Prospects in China's Three Economies: Mainland, Taiwan and Hong Kong', Monash University, Melbourne.

FORSTER, K. (1991), "China's Tea War", Chinese Economy Research Unit Working Paper No. 91/3, June.

GOLDSTEIN, M., and M. KHAN (1985), "Income and Price Elasticities in International Trade", in R. Jones and P. Kenen, eds, *Handbook of International Economics* (Elsevier Science Publications).

GRAIS, W., J. DE MELO, and S. URATA (1986), "A General Equilibrium Estimation of the Effect of Reduction in Tariffs and Quantitative Restrictions in Turkey in 1978", in T. Srinivasan and J. Whalley, eds, *General Equilibrium Trade Policy Modelling* (Massachusetts Institute of Technology Press, Cambridge).

GRIFFIN, K. (ed.) (1984), *Institutional Reform and Economic Development in the Chinese Countryside*, London, Macmillan.

GUNASEKERA, D., N. ANDREWS, H. HASZLER, J. CHAPMAN, TIAN WEIMING, and ZHAO ZHAO (1991), *Agricultural Policy Reform in China*, Discussion Paper 91.4, Australian Bureau of Agricultural and Resource Economics, Canberra.

GUO SHUTIAN (ed.) (1990), *Zhongguo Nongcun Gaige yu Fazhan Shi Nian*, [Ten years of reform and development in the Chinese countryside], Beijing, Nongye Chubanshe.

GUO SHUTIAN (ed.) (1990a), *Zhongguo Nongcun Gaige yu Fazhan Shi Nian*, [Ten Years of reform and development in the Chinese countryside], Beijing, Nongye Chubanshe.

GUO SHUTIAN (ed.) (1990b), *Zhongguo Liangshi: Duo jiaodu yanjiu yu sikao,* [China's grain: A multi-faceted approach to research and analysis], Beijing Nongye Chubanshe.

GUO SHUTIAN (ed.) (1991), *Nong chanpin jiage gaige shi zai bi xing*, [Reform of agricultural product prices is imperative], *Zhongguo Wujia,* [China Prices], No. 6, pp. 18-20.

HAN WEIRONG (1990), *Wo guo nong chanpin jiage gaige de fangxiang shi shichanghua ma?*, [Is the orientation of price reform for agricultural products in China towards the market?], *Zhongguo Wujia,* [China Prices], No. 8, pp. 12-16.

HUANG XIYUAN, ZHANG MINGHE, and YUAN BOTAO (1985), "Lun nongcun jizi wenti", [On the question of rural accumulation], *Nongye Jingji Wenti*, [Problems in Agricultural Economics], No. 8, p. 30.

INTERNATIONAL CURRENCY ANALYSIS (1989), *1988-89 World Currency Yearbook,* International Currency Analysis, Brooklyn, New York.

LAN GENGYUN (1991), "Quan guo nongcun zijin wenti taolunhui zongshu", [A summary of the national conference on rural capital funds], *Jingjixue Dongtai,* [Trends in Economics], No. 1, pp. 13-16.

LARDY, N. (1983), *Agricultural in China's Modern Economic Development,* London, Cambridge University Press.

LARDY, N. (1992), *Economic Reform in China, 1978-1990,* New York, Cambridge University Press.

LEAMER, E.E. (1987), "Paths of Development in the Three-Factor, n-Good General Equilibrium Model", *Journal of Political Economy*, 95(5), pp. 961-99.

LEAMER, E., and R. STERN (1970), *Quantitative International Economics* (Allyn and Bacon, Boston).

LI JI (1989), "Shoudu shucai pifa shichang kaocha", [A study of vegetable wholesale marketing in the capital], *Beijing Shang-Xueyuan Xuebao,* [Bulletin of the Beijing Institute of Commerce], No. 2 , pp. 56-61.

LI QINGZENG (1991), "Government Control of Grain Production in China", Chinese Economy Research Unit No. 91/10, University of Adelaide.

LIMSKUL, K. (1988), "The Sectoral Capital Stock, Employment and Sources of Economic Growth in Thailand: 1960-86", International Economic Conflict Discussion Paper No. 40 (Economic Research Center, Nagoya University).

LIN, JUSTIN (1989), "Rural Reforms and Agricultural Productivity Growth in China", UCLA Working Paper No. 576, December.

LIU XIANDAO (1984), "Shiying shangpin shengchan xuyao jianli nongcun nongfu chanpin pifa shichang", [It is necessary to establish rural product wholesale markets to suit commodity production], *Nongye Jingji Wenti,* [Problems in Agricultural Economics], No. 7, pp. 38-40.

LLUCH, C., A. POWELL, and R. WILLIAMS (1977), *Patterns in Household Demand and Savings* (Oxford University Press, Oxford).

LU BAIFU, and YUAN ZHENYU (1983), "Guanyu dangqian nong-fu chanpin shougou zhong de jige wenti", [Some current problems in the purchase of agricultural products], *Jingji Yanjiu,* [Economics Research], No. 5, pp. 65-69.

MA HONG (ed.) (1982), *Xiandai Zhongguo Jingji Shidian,* [An encyclopedia of the contemporary Chinese economy], Beijing, Zhongguo Shehui Kexue Chubanshe.

MAO YUFEI (1986), "Guanyu nongchanpin de xubei wenti", [On the question of stocks of agricultural products], *Caimao Jingji,* [Finance and Trade Economics], No. 8, pp. 58-60.

MARTIN, W. (1991a), "Modeling the Post-reform Chinese Economy", mimeo, World Bank, Washington, D.C.

MARTIN, W. (1991b), "China's Foreign Exchange System", mimeo, World Bank, Washington, D.C.

MARTIN, W. (1992), "Analysing the Effects of China's Exchange System on the Market for Wool", in C. Findlay, ed., *Challenges of Economic Reform and Industrial Growth: China's Wool War*, Allen and Unwin, Sydney.

MARTIN, W., and P. WARR (1992), "The Declining Importance of Agriculture: a Supply Side Analysis for Thailand", Working papers in Trade and Development, 92/1, Department of Economics and National Centre for Development Studies, Australian National University, Canberra.

McMILLAN, J., J. WHALLEY, and ZHU LIJING (1989), "The Impact of China's Economic Reforms on Agricultural Productivity Growth", *Journal of Political Economy*, August.

NICKUM, J. E. (1978), "Labour Accumulation in Rural China and its Role since the Cultural Revolution", *Cambridge Journal of Economics*, Vol. 2, September, pp. 273-86.

NONGCUN FAZHAN YANJIUSUO (1985), *Nong Chanpin Pifa Shichang Yanjiu*, [Studies of Wholesale Markets for Agricultural Products], Bejing, Nongcun Fazhan Yanjiusuo.

ROBINSON, S. (1989), "Multisectoral Models of Developing Countries: A Survey", in H. Chenery and T. Srinivasan, eds, *Handbook of Development Economics* (North Holland, Amsterdam).

RURAL ECONOMY SURVEY GROUP (1986), *Nongmin Ribao*, [Peasants' Daily], 7-20 May, also reprinted in *Nongye Jingji Wenti*, [Problems in Agricultural Economics], No. 6, pp. 4-13.

SALTER, W. (1959), "Internal and External Balance: the Role of Price and Expenditure Effects", *Economic Record*, 35, pp. 226-38.

SHANG ZHENGYUAN (1982), "Conscientiously Grasp Grain Work, Rationally Control Rural Sales", *Jingjixue Zhoubao*, [Economics Weekly], 27 December, pp. 1 and 3.

SHENG YUMING (1991), *Intersectoral Resource Flows in Development Economics: The Chinese Case*, London, Macmillan.

SHENG YUMING, LIU YUMAN, C. FINDLAY, and A. WATSON (1990), "The Political Economy of Agricultural Marketing in China: The Hog Reform Cycle", mimeo, Chinese Economy Research Unit, University of Adelaide, July.

SICULAR, T. (1988), "The Plan and Market in China's Agricultural Commerce", *Journal of Political Economy*, 96(2), pp. 383-7.

SICULAR, T. (1990), "China's Agricultural Policy During the Reform Period", Harvard Institute of Economic Research, Discussion Paper No. 1522, December.

SSB (State Statistical Bureau) (1983), *Zhongguo Tongji Nianjian 1983*, [China Statistical Yearbook 1983], Hong Kong, Jingji Daobao Chubanshe.

SSB (1986), *Zhongguo Nongcun Tongji Nianjian 1985*, [China's Rural Statistics Yearbook 1985], Beijing, Zhongguo Tongji Chubanshe.

SSB (1990), *Zhongguo Tongji Nianjian 1990*, [China Statistical Yearbook 1990], Beijing, Zhongguo Tongji Chubanshe.

SSB (1991), *Zhongguo Tongjl Zhaiyao 1990*, [Abstract of the Statistical Yearbook of China], Beijing.

STATE COUNCIL (1983), "Methods for the Management of Urban and Rural Market Trade", published in *Zhongguo Nongmin Bao*, [China Peasant Daily], 24 February, p. 2. A translation is available in *Summary of World Broadcasts*, Part 3, The Far East, FE/7270/BII/3-9, 1 March 1983.

STATE COUNCIL RESEARCH UNIT RURAL ECONOMY GROUP, and THE RURAL DEVELOPMENT RESEARCH INSTITUTE OF THE CHINESE ACADEMY OF SOCIAL SCIENCES (eds) (1990), *Bie Wu Xuanze - Xiangzhen Qiye yu Guomin Jingji de Xietiao Fazhan,* [There is a choice - the co-ordinated development of rural enterprises and the national economy], Beijing, Gaige Chubanshe.

STATE INDUSTRIAL AND COMMERCIAL ADMINISTRATION BUREAU (1984), "Wo guo cheng-xiang jishi maoyi riyi fanrong xingwang", [Market trade in China's towns and countryside steadily grows more prosperous], *Jingji Ribao* [Economics Daily], 11 July, p. 2.

SU XING (1979), "Nong chanpin jiage wenti", [Problems of agricultural product prices], *Shehui Kexue Zhanxian,* [Social Sciences Front], No. 2, pp. 101-8.

TAM ON-KIT (1988), "Rural Finance in China", *The China Quarterly,* No. 113, March, pp. 60-76.

TARR, D. (1989), "A General Equilibrium Analysis of the Welfare and Employment Effects of US Quotas in Textiles, Autos and Steel", Bureau of Economics Staff Report to the Federal Trade Commission, Washington.

THOMPSON, D. (1990), "Construction of a Consistent Market Price Data Base for a General Equilibrium Model of the Chinese Economy", China Working Paper 90/2 (National Centre for Development Studies, Australian National University, Canberra).

WARR, P., and ZHANG XIAOGUANG (1990), "Chinese Trade Pattern and Comparative Advantage", paper presented to the Chinese Students Society for Economic Studies, Third Conference, Macquarie University, November.

WATSON, A. (1984), "Agriculture Looks for 'Shoes that Fit': the Production Responsibility System and its Implications", in N. Maxwell and B. McFarlane, eds, *China's Changed Road to Development,* Oxford, Pergamon Press, pp. 83-108.

WATSON, A. (1985), "New Structures in the Organization of Chinese Agriculture: A Variable Model", *Pacific Affairs,* Vol. 57, No. 4, pp. 621-45.

WATSON, A. (1988), "The Reform of Agricultural Marketing in China since 1978", *The China Quarterly,* No. 113, March, pp. 1-28.

WATSON, A. (1989), "Investment Issues in the Chinese Countryside", *The Australian Journal of Chinese Affairs,* No. 22, July, pp. 85-126.

WATSON, A. (1991a), "Working Paper on Forestry Production and Marketing in China", paper presented to the Chinese Economy Research Unit seminar on "Agricultural Marketing in China and Rural Economic Development", University of Adelaide, 27 June.

WATSON, A. (1991b), "Conflict over Cabbages: The Reform of Wholesale Marketing in China", paper presented to the Chinese Economy Research Unit seminar on "Agricultural Marketing in China and Rural Economic Development", University of Adelaide, 27 June.

WATSON, A. (1992), "The Management of the Rural Economy: The Institutional Parameters", in Watson, A., ed., *Economic Reform and Social Change in China,* London, Routledge, pp. 171-99.

WATSON, A., C. FINDLAY, and DU YINTANG (1989), "Who Won the 'Wool War'?: A Case Study of Rural Product Marketing in China", *The China Quarterly,* No. 118, June, pp. 213-41.

WEBB, SHWU-ENG, H. (1991), "China's Agricultural Commodity Policies in the 1980s", mimeo, Economic Research Service, USDA

WEBB, SHWU-ENG, H., and FRANCIS C. TUAN (1991), "China's Agricultural Reforms: Evaluation and Outlook", in *China's Economic Dilemmas in the 1990s: The Problems of Reforms, Modernization, and Interependence,* Volume 1, Study papers presented to the Joint Economic Committee of the Congress of the United States.

WEI YALING (1986), "Nong chanpin pifa shichang riyi xingwang", [Wholesale markets for agricultural products continue to thrive], *Renmin Ribao,* [People's Daily], 11 June, p. 2.

WORLD BANK (1985a), "China: Economic Structure in International Perspective", Annex 5 to *China's Long-Term Development Issues and Options,* (World Bank, Washington, D.C).

WORLD BANK (1985b), "China: Economic Model and Projections", Annex 4 to *China's Long Term Development Issues and Options,* (World Bank, Washington, D.C).

WORLD BANK (1985c), "China: Agriculture to the year 2000", Annex 2 to *China's Long Term Development Issues and Options,* (World Bank, Washington, D.C).

WORLD BANK (1987), *China: The Livestock Sector,* World Bank, Washington, D.C.

WORLD BANK (1988), *China: External Trade and Capital,* September, World Bank, Washington, D.C.

WORLD BANK (1990a), "Grain Marketing, Price Policy and Foreign Trade", *Managing an Agricultural Transformation,* Part 1, Grain Sector Review, Working papers, No. 7.

WORLD BANK (1990b), "Grain Production Prospects and Constraints", Working Paper No. 4, Grain Sector Review, Part 1 of *Managing an Agricultural Transformation.*

WU JINGLIAN, and ZHAO RENWEI (1987), "The Dual Pricing System in China's Industry", Journal of Comparative Economics, 11(3), pp. 309-18.

WU SHUO (1980), "Yunyong jiazhi guilu, heli tiaozheng nong chanpin shougou jiage", [Use the law of value, rationally adjust the purchase prices for agricultural products] in Jingji Yanjiu, ed., *Guanyu Wo Guo Jingji Guanli Tizhi Gaige de Tantao,* [Explorations of the reform of China's system of economic management], Shandong, Renmin Chubanshe.

WU SHUO, and YANG MIN (1991), "Liangshi liutong zouchu kunjing de duice yanjiu", [Research on the appropriate policies to liberate grain circulation from its current difficulties], *Nongye Jingji Wenti,* [Problems in Agricultural Economics], No. 2, pp. 8-14.

YANG SHENGMING (1990), "Nong chanpin jiage 'gaige bing' de zhenzhi", [The cure for "reform sickness" in the prices for agricultural products], *Zhongguo Wujia,* [China Prices], No. 8, pp. 17-22.

YANG YONGZHENG, and R. TYERS (1989), "The Economic Costs of Food Self-Sufficiency in China", *World Development,* 17(2), pp. 237-53.

YIN SANQIANG (1990), "Nongye zijin touru bu zu de yuan fenxi", [An analysis of the causes of insufficient investment funds in agriculture], *Jingji Cankao,* [Economic Reference], 25 December, p. 4.

ZHANG LIUZHENG (1974), "Fazhan nongye shengchan, gaishan nongmin shenghuo", [Develop agricultural production, improve the peasants' standard of living], *Nongye Jingji Wenti,* [Problems in Agricultural Economics], No. 1, pp. 33-5.

ZHANG LIUZHENG (1985), "Jin yibu fazhan nong chanpin pifa shichang de ruogan wenti", [Some issues in the further development of wholesale markets for agricultural products], *Nongye Jingji Wenti,* [Problems in Agricultural Economics], No. 12, pp. 41-43.

ZHANG QUANXIN (1986), "Nong chanpin pifa shichang yanjiu", [A study of wholesale markets for agricultural products], *Zhongguo Nongcun Jingji,* [China's Rural Economy], No. 2, pp. 42-45.

ZHANG XIAOHE (1991a), "The Urban-Rural Isolation Policy and its Impact on China's Production and Trade Pattern", Chinese Economy Research Unit Working Paper No. 91/4 University of Adelaide.

ZHANG XIAOHE (1991b), "The Classification of China's Industries by Factor Intensity and the Corresponding Trade Pattern of China", Chinese Economy Research Unit Working Paper No. 91/1, University of Adelaide.

ZHANG XIAOHE (1991c), "China's Textile Industry and Cotton Production", paper presented to the Chinese Economy Research Unit seminar on "Agricultural Marketing in China and Rural Economic Development", University of Adelaide, 27 June.

ZHANG ZHICHENG, and WANG QIHUA (1979), "Cong nong-fu chanpinb de shougou zhengce kan jihua tiejie he shichang tiaojie de guanxi", [The relationship between plan regulation and market regulation seen from the perspective of agricultural product purchasing policy], *Jingji Yanjiu*, [Economics Research], No. 6, pp. 70-74.

ZHAO XINGHAN (1984), "Nong chanpin jiage xingcheng jichu tantao", [An exploration of the basis of price formation in agricultural products], *Jingji Yanjiu*, [Economics Research], No. 3, pp. 45-49.

ZHAO ZIYANG (1985), "Fangkai nong chanpin jiage cujin nongcun chanye jiegou de tiaozheng", [Loosen control over the prices of farm products to promote the readjustment of the production structure in the rural areas], *Renmin Ribao*, [People's Daily], 31 January, p. 1.

ZHONG MING (1990), "Quan guo nong chanpin jiage lilun taolunhui zongshu", [A summary of the national conference on agricultural product prices]. *Jingjixue Dongtai*, [Trends in Economics], No. 9, pp. 13-16

ZHONGGUO JINGJI NIANJIAN BIANJI WEIYUANHUI (1983), *Zhongguo Jingji Nianjian 1983* [China Economic Yearbook 1983], Beijing, Jingji Guanli Zazhi Chubanshe.

ZHONGGUO NONGYE NIANJIAN BIANJI WEIYUANHUI (1983), *Zhongguo Nongye Nianjian 1982*, [China Agricultural Yearbook 1982], Beijing, Nongye Chubanshe.

ZHONGGUO NONGYE NIANJIAN BIANJI WEIYUANHUI (1984), *Zhongguo Nongye Nianjian 1983*, [China Agricultural Yearbook 1983], Beijing, Nongye Chubanshe.

ZHU MIN (1989), "1988 nian jiage gaige qingkuang jianshu", [A brief outline of price reform in 1988], *Jiage Lilun yu Shijian*, [Price Theory and Practice], No. 4, pp. 19-23.

ZOU SHULIN (1987), "Wo guo nongye chixu zengzhang de yanjiu", [Research on sustained growth in China's agriculture], *Jingji Wenti Tansuo*, [Inquiry into Economic Problems], No. 1, p. 12.

ZUO ZHAOYI (1984), "Chongqingshi nongmao shichang diaocha", [A survey of agricultural markets in Chongqing], *Nongye Jingji Wenti*, [Problems in Agricultural Economics], No. 12, pp. 9-13.

MAIN SALES OUTLETS OF OECD PUBLICATIONS
PRINCIPAUX POINTS DE VENTE DES PUBLICATIONS DE L'OCDE

ARGENTINA – ARGENTINE
Carlos Hirsch S.R.L.
Galería Güemes, Florida 165, 4° Piso
1333 Buenos Aires Tel. (1) 331.1787 y 331.2391
Telefax: (1) 331.1787

AUSTRALIA – AUSTRALIE
D.A. Information Services
648 Whitehorse Road, P.O.B 163
Mitcham, Victoria 3132 Tel. (03) 873.4411
Telefax: (03) 873.5679

AUSTRIA – AUTRICHE
Gerold & Co.
Graben 31
Wien I Tel. (0222) 533.50.14

BELGIUM – BELGIQUE
Jean De Lannoy
Avenue du Roi 202
B-1060 Bruxelles Tel. (02) 538.51.69/538.08.41
Telefax: (02) 538.08.41

CANADA
Renouf Publishing Company Ltd.
1294 Algoma Road
Ottawa, ON K1B 3W8 Tel. (613) 741.4333
Telefax: (613) 741.5439
Stores:
61 Sparks Street
Ottawa, ON K1P 5R1 Tel. (613) 238.8985
211 Yonge Street
Toronto, ON M5B 1M4 Tel. (416) 363.3171
Telefax: (416)363.59.63

Les Éditions La Liberté Inc.
3020 Chemin Sainte-Foy
Sainte-Foy, PQ G1X 3V6 Tel. (418) 658.3763
Telefax: (418) 658.3763

Federal Publications
165 University Avenue
Toronto, ON M5H 3B8 Tel. (416) 581.1552
Telefax: (416) 581.1743

Les Publications Fédérales
1185 Avenue de l'Université
Montréal, PQ H3B 3A7 Tel. (514) 954.1633
Telefax : (514) 954.1633

CHINA – CHINE
China National Publications Import
Export Corporation (CNPIEC)
16 Gongti E. Road, Chaoyang District
P.O. Box 88 or 50
Beijing 100704 PR Tel. (01) 506.6688
Telefax: (01) 506.3101

DENMARK – DANEMARK
Munksgaard Export and Subscription Service
35, Nørre Søgade, P.O. Box 2148
DK-1016 København K Tel. (33) 12.85.70
Telefax: (33) 12.93.87

FINLAND – FINLANDE
Akateeminen Kirjakauppa
Keskuskatu 1, P.O. Box 128
00100 Helsinki Tel. (358 0) 12141
Telefax: (358 0) 121.4441

FRANCE
OECD/OCDE
Mail Orders/Commandes par correspondance:
2, rue André-Pascal
75775 Paris Cedex 16 Tel. (33-1) 45.24.82.00
Telefax: (33-1) 45.24.81.76 or (33-1) 45.24.85.00
Telex: 640048 OCDE

OECD Bookshop/Librairie de l'OCDE :
33, rue Octave-Feuillet
75016 Paris Tel. (33-1) 45.24.81.67
(33-1) 45.24.81.81

Documentation Française
29, quai Voltaire
75007 Paris Tel. 40.15.70.00

Gibert Jeune (Droit-Économie)
6, place Saint-Michel
75006 Paris Tel. 43.25.91.19

Librairie du Commerce International
10, avenue d'Iéna
75016 Paris Tel. 40.73.34.60

Librairie Dunod
Université Paris-Dauphine
Place du Maréchal de Lattre de Tassigny
75016 Paris Tel. 47.27.18.56

Librairie Lavoisier
11, rue Lavoisier
75008 Paris Tel. 42.65.39.95

Librairie L.G.D.J. - Montchrestien
20, rue Soufflot
75005 Paris Tel. 46.33.89.85

Librairie des Sciences Politiques
30, rue Saint-Guillaume
75007 Paris Tel. 45.48.36.02

P.U.F.
49, boulevard Saint-Michel
75005 Paris Tel. 43.25.83.40

Librairie de l'Université
12a, rue Nazareth
13100 Aix-en-Provence Tel. (16) 42.26.18.08

Documentation Française
165, rue Garibaldi
69003 Lyon Tel. (16) 78.63.32.23

Librairie Decitre
29, place Bellecour
69002 Lyon Tel. (16) 72.40.54.54

GERMANY – ALLEMAGNE
OECD Publications and Information Centre
August-Bebel-Allee 6
D-W 5300 Bonn 2 Tel. (0228) 959.120
Telefax: (0228) 959.12.17

GREECE – GRÈCE
Librairie Kauffmann
Mavrokordatou 9
106 78 Athens Tel. 322.21.60
Telefax: 363.39.67

HONG-KONG
Swindon Book Co. Ltd.
13–15 Lock Road
Kowloon, Hong Kong Tel. 366.80.31
Telefax: 739.49.75

HUNGARY – HONGRIE
Euro Info Service
POB 1271
1464 Budapest Tel. (1) 111.62.16
Telefax : (1) 111.60.61

ICELAND – ISLANDE
Mál Mog Menning
Laugavegi 18, Pósthólf 392
121 Reykjavik Tel. 162.35.23

INDIA – INDE
Oxford Book and Stationery Co.
Scindia House
New Delhi 110001 Tel.(11) 331.5896/5308
Telefax: (11) 332.5993

17 Park Street
Calcutta 700016 Tel. 240832

INDONESIA – INDONÉSIE
Pdii-Lipi
P.O. Box 269/JKSMG/88
Jakarta 12790 Tel. 583467
Telex: 62 875

IRELAND – IRLANDE
TDC Publishers – Library Suppliers
12 North Frederick Street
Dublin 1 Tel. 74.48.35/74.96.77
Telefax: 74.84.16

ISRAEL
Electronic Publications only
Publications électroniques seulement
Sophist Systems Ltd.
71 Allenby Street
Tel-Aviv 65134 Tel. 3-29.00.21
Telefax: 3-29.92.39

ITALY – ITALIE
Libreria Commissionaria Sansoni
Via Duca di Calabria 1/1
50125 Firenze Tel. (055) 64.54.15
Telefax: (055) 64.12.57

Via Bartolini 29
20155 Milano Tel. (02) 36.50.83

Editrice e Libreria Herder
Piazza Montecitorio 120
00186 Roma Tel. 679.46.28
Telefax: 678.47.51

Libreria Hoepli
Via Hoepli 5
20121 Milano Tel. (02) 86.54.46
Telefax: (02) 805.28.86

Libreria Scientifica
Dott. Lucio de Biasio 'Aeiou'
Via Coronelli, 6
20146 Milano Tel. (02) 48.95.45.52
Telefax: (02) 48.95.45.48

JAPAN – JAPON
OECD Publications and Information Centre
Landic Akasaka Building
2-3-4 Akasaka, Minato-ku
Tokyo 107 Tel. (81.3) 3586.2016
Telefax: (81.3) 3584.7929

KOREA – CORÉE
Kyobo Book Centre Co. Ltd.
P.O. Box 1658, Kwang Hwa Moon
Seoul Tel. 730.78.91
Telefax: 735.00.30

MALAYSIA – MALAISIE
Co-operative Bookshop Ltd.
University of Malaya
P.O. Box 1127, Jalan Pantai Baru
59700 Kuala Lumpur
Malaysia Tel. 756.5000/756.5425
Telefax: 757.3661

MEXICO – MEXIQUE
Revistas y Periodicos Internacionales S.A. de C.V.
Florencia 57 - 1004
Mexico, D.F. 06600 Tel. 207.81.00
Telefax : 208.39.79

NETHERLANDS – PAYS-BAS
SDU Uitgeverij
Christoffel Plantijnstraat 2
Postbus 20014
2500 EA's-Gravenhage Tel. (070 3) 78.99.11
Voor bestellingen: Tel. (070 3) 78.98.80
Telefax: (070 3) 47.63.51

NEW ZEALAND
NOUVELLE-ZÉLANDE
Legislation Services
P.O. Box 12418
Thorndon, Wellington Tel. (04) 496.5652
Telefax: (04) 496.5698

NORWAY – NORVÈGE
Narvesen Info Center – NIC
Bertrand Narvesens vei 2
P.O. Box 6125 Etterstad
0602 Oslo 6 Tel. (02) 57.33.00
Telefax: (02) 68.19.01

PAKISTAN
Mirza Book Agency
65 Shahrah Quaid-E-Azam
Lahore 54000 Tel. (42) 353.601
Telefax: (42) 231.730

PHILIPPINE – PHILIPPINES
International Book Center
5th Floor, Filipinas Life Bldg.
Ayala Avenue
Metro Manila Tel. 81.96.76
Telex 23312 RHP PH

PORTUGAL
Livraria Portugal
Rua do Carmo 70-74
Apart. 2681
1117 Lisboa Codex Tel.: (01) 347.49.82/3/4/5
Telefax: (01) 347.02.64

SINGAPORE – SINGAPOUR
Information Publications Pte. Ltd.
41, Kallang Pudding, No. 04-03
Singapore 1334 Tel. 741.5166
Telefax: 742.9356

SPAIN – ESPAGNE
Mundi-Prensa Libros S.A.
Castelló 37, Apartado 1223
Madrid 28001 Tel. (91) 431.33.99
Telefax: (91) 575.39.98

Libreria Internacional AEDOS
Consejo de Ciento 391
08009 – Barcelona Tel. (93) 488.34.92
Telefax: (93) 487.76.59

Llibreria de la Generalitat
Palau Moja
Rambla dels Estudis, 118
08002 – Barcelona
(Subscripcions) Tel. (93) 318.80.12
(Publicacions) Tel. (93) 302.67.23
Telefax: (93) 412.18.54

SRI LANKA
Centre for Policy Research
c/o Colombo Agencies Ltd.
No. 300-304, Galle Road
Colombo 3 Tel. (1) 574240, 573551-2
Telefax: (1) 575394, 510711

SWEDEN – SUÈDE
Fritzes Fackboksföretaget
Box 16356
Regeringsgatan 12
103 27 Stockholm Tel. (08) 690.90.90
Telefax: (08) 20.50.21

Subscription Agency-Agence d'abonnements
Wennergren-Williams AB
P.O. Box 1305
171 25 Solna Tel. (08) 705.97.50
Téléfax : (08) 27.00.71

SWITZERLAND – SUISSE
Maditec S.A. (Books and Periodicals - Livres et périodiques)
Chemin des Palettes 4
Case postale 2066
1020 Renens 1 Tel. (021) 635.08.65
Telefax: (021) 635.07.80

Librairie Payot S.A.
4, place Pépinet
1003 Lausanne Tel. (021) 341.33.48
Telefax: (021) 341.33.45

Librairie Unilivres
6, rue de Candolle
1205 Genève Tel. (022) 320.26.23
Telefax: (022) 329.73.18

Subscription Agency - Agence d'abonnement
Dynapresse Marketing S.A.
38 avenue Vibert
1227 Carouge Tel.: (022) 308.07.89
Telefax : (022) 308.07.99

See also – Voir aussi :
OECD Publications and Information Centre
August-Bebel-Allee 6
D-W 5300 Bonn 2 (Germany) Tel. (0228) 959.120
Telefax: (0228) 959.12.17

TAIWAN – FORMOSE
Good Faith Worldwide Int'l. Co. Ltd.
9th Floor, No. 118, Sec. 2
Chung Hsiao E. Road
Taipei Tel. (02) 391.7396/391.7397
Telefax: (02) 394.9176

THAILAND – THAÏLANDE
Suksit Siam Co. Ltd.
113, 115 Fuang Nakhon Rd.
Opp. Wat Rajbopith
Bangkok 10200 Tel. (662) 251.1630
Telefax: (662) 236.7783

TURKEY – TURQUIE
Kültür Yayinlari Is-Türk Ltd. Sti.
Atatürk Bulvari No. 191/Kat 13
Kavaklidere/Ankara Tel. 428.11.40 Ext. 2458
Dolmabahce Cad. No. 29
Besiktas/Istanbul Tel. 260.71.88
Telex: 43482B

UNITED KINGDOM – ROYAUME-UNI
HMSO
Gen. enquiries Tel. (071) 873 0011
Postal orders only:
P.O. Box 276, London SW8 5DT
Personal Callers HMSO Bookshop
49 High Holborn, London WC1V 6HB
Telefax: (071) 873 8200
Branches at: Belfast, Birmingham, Bristol, Edinburgh, Manchester

UNITED STATES – ÉTATS-UNIS
OECD Publications and Information Centre
2001 L Street N.W., Suite 700
Washington, D.C. 20036-4910 Tel. (202) 785.6323
Telefax: (202) 785.0350

VENEZUELA
Libreria del Este
Avda F. Miranda 52, Aptdo. 60337
Edificio Galipán
Caracas 106 Tel. 951.1705/951.2307/951.1297
Telegram: Libreste Caracas

Subscription to OECD periodicals may also be placed through main subscription agencies.

Les abonnements aux publications périodiques de l'OCDE peuvent être souscrits auprès des principales agences d'abonnement.

Orders and inquiries from countries where Distributors have not yet been appointed should be sent to: OECD Publications Service, 2 rue André-Pascal, 75775 Paris Cedex 16, France.

Les commandes provenant de pays où l'OCDE n'a pas encore désigné de distributeur devraient être adressées à : OCDE, Service des Publications, 2, rue André-Pascal, 75775 Paris Cedex 16, France.

04-1993

OECD PUBLICATIONS, 2 rue André-Pascal, 75775 PARIS CEDEX 16
PRINTED IN FRANCE
(41 93 04 1) ISBN 92-64-13907-9 - No. 46443 1993